The
Papal
Year

Peter Hebblethwaite

Waterloo 9 May 84

The Papal Year

Peter Hebblethwaite

Geoffrey Chapman · London

A Geoffrey Chapman book published by
Cassell Ltd.
35 Red Lion Square, London WC1R 4SG
and at Sydney, Auckland, Toronto, Johannesburg,
an affiliate of
Macmillan Publishing Co. Inc.,
New York

First published 1981
ISBN 0 225 66297 3

British Library Cataloguing in Publication Data
Hebblethwaite, Peter

The Papal Year
1. Papacy–History–20th century
I. Title
262'.13'09047   BX1390

Printed and bound in Great Britain at
The Camelot Press Ltd, Southampton

Contents

Grateful acknowledgements to the following for pictures:

Arturo Mari of L'Osservatore Romano, Vatican
8, 9, 10, 12, 14, 17 top, 19, 20, 21, 22, 23, 24, 25, 27, 28, 30, 32, 33, 38, 41, 42, 43, 46, 51, 63, 65, 67, 68, 69, 70 top, 73 left, 76, 81, 85, 90, 91, 92, 93, 97, 98, 99

Frank Spooner Pictures (Photo Gamma)
18 left, 54, 57, 64, 71, 72, 79, 82, 83, 84, 89, 94, 100, 106, 110, 111, 112, 115, 119, 120, 122, 123, front and back cover

Camera Press
13, 26, 77, 87, 126

Popperfoto
11, 29, 37, 58, 61, 62, 66, 70 bottom

Roma Press Photo
16, 35, 50 right

Associated Press
18 right, 44, 55, 56, 73 right, 80, 96

Keystone
17 bottom, 49 right

Press Association
74, 101, 104

William Collins Sons & Co Ltd
49 left, 50 left

Grateful thanks also to The Universe and The Catholic Herald for assistance with research

Picture Research by Linda Proud
Designed by Carole Griffin

This is a picture book with a difference. The difference is that the text has importance in its own right, and that the pictures fill out what it has to say. For the first time we have an objective analysis of the John Paul II phenomenon. He has travelled the world, gathered millions almost everywhere: but what does it all mean for the RC Church, for Christians generally, and for the world?

Peter Hebblethwaite is uniquely placed to answer these questions. Theologian, scholar, linguist, he is author of a series of books on the Vatican including *The Runaway Church* and *The Year of the Three Popes*. He is now the Vatican Affairs correspondent of the *National Catholic Reporter* (published in Kansas City). Based in Rome, he has recently been elected President of CCIR, the Cultural Centre for Religious Information.

1 A Crowded Year

Brazil – the most arduous journey in
a remarkable year of papal travel . . .

1980 was a truly astonishing papal year in sheer output and
display of charismatic energy. No pope has ever before
attempted to cover so much ground, in every sense of the term.
Keeping up with the volume of words is a major and daunting
undertaking. This became obvious to the world during the
spectacular journeys. But even when apparently staying quietly
at home in the Vatican, John Paul regularly produces two or
three speeches a day. No audience is too insignificant for a brief
address. He has spoken to hairdressers ('your profession is

8

essentially a service'), motorway policemen, florists, sportsmen, quarrymen, Rome conservationists—and without claiming the universal expertise of Pope Pius XII, he has had a personal message for each group.

Besides the speeches and the sermons, there have been countless telegrams, letters and messages. The anniversaries of St Basil, St Benedict and St Catherine of Siena have been duly celebrated with documents. The letter to the German bishops, commending them for the way they handled the Hans Küng affair, amounts to a mini-treatise on infallibility. The message

. . . but returning to the central theme of 'the gift beyond price'.

for World Peace Day (1 January) contained blunt advice to politicians on telling the truth. The lengthy letter to the world's bishops (*Inaestimabile Donum*, published on Maundy Thursday) praised liturgical reform, recommended the survival of the Latin Mass, and denounced a number of 'liturgical excesses'. Ghost writers can provide drafts and ease the literary burden, but almost every one of these texts has the characteristic stamp of John Paul's personal style.

Not only that, but in the year covered by this book, John Paul has made five major journeys outside Italy: to Turkey, to six African countries, to France, Brazil and West Germany. Africa and Brazil in particular were real marathons with almost daily flights from place to place, over seventy speeches, and no one getting to bed until well after midnight. Naturally enough, each of these journeys involved time for preparation and recovery. And so the criticism was inevitably heard: 'The Pope is travelling too much.'

Too much for whom? Certainly not for the people who have (with the single exception of Turkey) welcomed him in their hundreds of thousands. They have not complained at this unique opportunity to see the Pope in person. Previously you had to go to Rome to see the Pope. 'But the poor', as a Brazilian bishop explained, 'cannot afford to travel.' They cannot go to him, so John Paul has gone to them. Neither do the journalists accredited to the Vatican complain, for they see the world, admittedly in rather bizarre circumstances.

It seems, then, that the only people who complain about the papal journeys are the members of his staff, the Roman Curia. These long absences mean that their documents are not being studied, their memos remain unanswered, and that everything they have to refer to 'Higher Authority' (capital letters seem obligatory) remains in suspense. Of course no one actually says anything, but there are murmurings and an atmosphere.

The Pope among the poor, in a Brazilian shanty town.

John Paul has been sensitive to these muted criticisms. The proof is that he has answered them on at least two occasions. In an interview given conjointly to Vatican Radio and the *Osservatore Romano* he said: 'Many people say the pope is travelling too much and at too frequent intervals. Speaking from the human point of view, they are right'. He made it clear that such was not his point of view, for he went on: 'But it is Providence that guides me, and sometimes it suggests that we do certain things to excess' (*Osservatore Romano*, 13 June).

It is difficult to argue with Providence. Unofficially it is known that the papal doctor has proposed a more relaxed rhythm of work, on the grounds that in five years' time John Paul will be a burnt-out case. To this he replies that nobody knows what will

In the mid-day sun during an
outdoor Mass at Kinshasa, Zaire.

happen in five years' time and that meanwhile he has urgent
work to do.

In his address to the Roman Curia on 28 June, John Paul offered
a slightly different apologia for his travels. These journeys, he
said, are 'an authentic pilgrimage to the sanctuary of the living
People of God'. They are an expression of 'collegiality in action'.
'Collegiality', a key-term re-emphasized by the Second Vatican
Council (1962–65), means that the bishops of the world form a
team, 'with and under the Pope'. It means that they are
co-responsible for the universal Church.

There are many ways in which the sense of collegiality can be expressed: Roman synods (now every three years), the regular *ad limina* visits of bishops to Rome (every five years), and the meeting of the college of cardinals, revived in November 1979 by John Paul after a lapse of over four hundred years. All these involve going to Rome. But there can be movement the other way. The journeys can be justified as yet another expression of collegiality, one that has been made possible by 'modern means of communication', ie jet aircraft. The Pope said that SS. Peter and Paul would have used this apostolic method if it had been available to them (television, too, one might add).

Only one of many flights during the Pope's visit to Brazil.

The apologetic note was even clearer when John Paul claimed that he was not an innovator: 'John XXIII had foreseen this development, Paul VI gave it full realisation on a vast scale, and John Paul I would certainly have developed it still further.' No doubt. But Paul VI, who stopped travelling after 1970 when he went to the Far East, could not have imagined the sheer energy that a youngish pope, 58 when elected, would bring to this apostolic task. We now have a travelling papacy, a missionary pope, a pope who wants to see for himself what is happening in the local Churches which make up the 'diversified unity' that is called the Roman Catholic Church.

But the journeys, spectacular and colourful though they are, should not blind us to the fact that John Paul has sought to take a firm grip on the Church of which he is, very self-consciously, the leader. Though I do not accept the right-wing thesis that Paul VI was a wishy-washy liberal who could not make up his mind and who, Hamlet-like, preferred to hedge his bets, it is fairly obviously true that John Paul's style of leadership is very different. It is marked by clarity and firmness. It excludes hesitancy, doubt and self-questioning. His theme is 'the joy of faith in a troubled world' (the title of a chapter in his Apostolic Exhortation on catechesis). He wants to cheer up people, to restore their faith, to renew their hope and so to stimulate their charity. He believes that in the mystery of divine Providence, he, a Pole, was elected pope because Poland has suffered uniquely.

So Poland has a unique message to offer to the whole Catholic world and more especially to the rather tired West: do not flinch, do not give way to secularisation, do not lose heart before the inevitable challenges of the late-twentieth century. The attacks on the sacredness of the priesthood, the sanctity of marriage and the primacy of the spiritual can all be beaten off. The Church can only affect the world if order reigns within it.

It is in this perspective that the 'conservative' moves of John Paul should be seen and understood. He believes that Vatican II unleashed a crisis on the Church and that his God-given task is to overcome its potentially catastrophic effects. So he has strongly reaffirmed the importance and irreplaceability of the ordained ministry. He has said that without the doctrine of infallibility 'faith crumbles' (cf. his 'Letter to the German Bishops'). He has rejected the possibility of ordaining women. He has brought the Dutch Church, or at least the unfortunate Dutch bishops, to heel, and claimed that their fate is exemplary for the whole Church. He has dealt with allegedly errant theologians, and incurred a lot of odium in the process. He has

The Bishop of Rome in Nervi's huge modern audience hall in the Vatican.

13

not been afraid to denounce the 'consumerism' of the West as well as the lack of human rights in the East. He has reasserted, in striking and challenging form, Catholic *identity*. In other

A moment of splendour with the bishops of Brazil.

words, he has behaved surprisingly for a post-Vatican II pope, but not surprisingly for a Polish pope.

There are some who say that two and a half years is not a long enough period to judge a pontificate. That is true in the sense that we do not know how long the pontificate of John Paul will last—it could see us through to the year 2000, a date which possesses a peculiar fascination for the Pope. But the statement is false if it means that the first two years do not allow us to see at least the direction in which John Paul is moving and wants the Church to move.

His first year was full of surprises and apparently unrelated initiatives. The second year was marked by growing self-confidence on the part of the Pope, the consolidation of previous positions, and the emergence of a clear pattern. It is now established, for example, that the emphasis in ecumenism will fall on relations with the Orthodox Churches rather than the Churches which issued from the Reformation. It is by now undeniable that the halting of laicisations (or resignations from the priesthood) was not a temporary delay but a positive change of policy. John Paul's second year in office explained most of the puzzles of his first year and foreshadowed his third year. Of course there will be surprises, but they will occur within a known framework.

The plan of this book emerged naturally by considering the titles of the Pope. He is first of all the Bishop of Rome: so we begin in Rome and see him at work there. He is the Primate of Italy: so we look at the 'Italian dimension' next. Then he is the 'universal pastor', and this opens up the vast field of administration, 'running the Church', as well as contacts with other Christians. Finally come the journeys which are what interested the media and in which we see the 'universal pastor' interacting with important local Churches. The chronology of events has been respected, without turning the book into a diary.

For the sake of theological accuracy it should be added that the Pope is not the Church, and that the ecclesiastical history of the past year is not exhausted by this book—far from it. In the life of the Christian, the most important events happen off-stage,

Vatican walls do not a prisoner make.

where there is no reporter to record them. Yet to follow the Pope is to get a unique opportunity to grasp something of the present state of the Church in its international dimension. If one remembers those principles, then both superstitious papolatry and self-indulgent *lèse-papauté* can be avoided.

2   *The Pope at Home*

Blessing the crowds at the *Angelus* in April.

Receiving Mother Teresa.

John Paul II has left the Vatican more than any other pope in modern times. The statisticians report that he has set off, either by helicopter or in the Mercedes marked SCV 1, over a hundred times already. Unlike Pius IX, he cannot be described as 'the prisoner of the Vatican'. In Cracow he sometimes referred to his episcopal residence as 'the cage' and he escaped from it to the mountains as often as he could. Now his only escape to some sort of privacy is to retreat to the papal summer residence at Castelgandolfo. He has used it much more often than his predecessors, and used it all the year round.

Nevertheless the Vatican, and in particular the top floor of the Apostolic Palace, is his home and place of work. It is here that he welcomes guests, statesmen, friends, bishops from all over the world, members of the Roman Curia. Specially favoured friends are invited to the Pope's Mass at seven in the morning and they usually stay to talk over breakfast. It helps to be Polish. Others have slightly more formal private audiences. By definition they are secret. But we do know that Franz-Josef Strauss, leader of the Christian Democrats in West Germany, struck a blow for tradition by conversing with the Pope in Latin; and Norman St John Stevas, leader of the House of Commons in Britain, revealed that he had talked to the Pope about the problem of priests who wished to resign. The stream of visitors is constant, and since John Paul has not adopted the Italian habit of the siesta, he sometimes summons curial officials from their slumbers in the middle of the afternoon.

Still within the Vatican, there are the official meetings with a formal exchange of speeches. Ambassadors come along to present their credentials: in this year Greece, Jamaica and the People's Republic of the Congo have all established diplomatic relations with the Holy See, while Zimbabwe is about to do so. There was a state visit from the President of Portugal, General Antonio Eanes, on 16 May, and Queen Elizabeth II was received on 17 October. President Jimmy Carter dropped in by helicopter on 21 June on his way to a summit meeting in Venice. Daughter Amy did a lovely curtsey, and the Carter family spent half an hour with the Pope in his private library. Pope and President

Formality for Queen Elizabeth II, Supreme Governor of the Church of England.

An informal greeting for Amy Carter, as her father the President looks on.

joked about the difficulty of pronouncing the name of Kateri Tekakwitha, an American Indian girl, born in what is now the state of New York, who was to be beatified the next day.

With American Indians from the USA and Canada after the beatification on 22 June of Kateri Tekakwitha.

It would be a mistake to think of these meetings as purely formal affairs. That Greece should have diplomatic relations with the Holy See is important for ecumenism, for hitherto it was the Greek Orthodox Church that was most suspicious of the Vatican. Again, John Paul used the occasion of the visit of President Carter to make a serious point about Jerusalem: the city should have international status, and its future could not be decided unilaterally by the Israeli government. Christians and Moslems also had a stake in the city. So despite the burden of protocol, important business gets done.

Other pilgrims who flock to Rome in increasing numbers do not penetrate inside the Vatican. They usually see the Pope at the general audience which takes place regularly on Wednesdays. The time and place vary according to the weather or the season. In winter, audiences started at eleven in the morning. The pilgrims were divided into two groups: Italian speakers went inside St Peter's while other languages were accommodated in

19

Nervi's audience hall. In the spring the audiences moved outside into St Peter's Square. And in the summer, the time was changed to 5.30 pm in order, it was said, to make a gesture towards alleviating Rome's chronic traffic problems. What has not varied has been the vast numbers of people wanting to see the Pope and to have their children and rosaries blessed.

Children often caught the Pope's attention at general audiences.

So did the circus . . .

The general audiences, as developed by John Paul, are part religious rally, part lecture, part prayer and part entertainment. First of all the Pope, when in the Square, moves through the aisles in his pope-mobile, a white-painted jeep, for about half an hour. That is picture time. He then reads out his prepared speech which, throughout the year, has been an exposition of the opening chapters of the book of Genesis. This is in Italian, but John Paul next reads a summary of what he has just said in various European languages. After the blessing, the Pope speaks again, but this time more informally as he greets the various national groups that are present. There will always be a special word for the sick and the newly-wed. John Paul leads the singing of the 'Our Father'. What comes next is completely unpredictable. It depends who is there. But in the course of the

... which performed for him in the audience chamber in February.

year pop groups have twanged and hollered, choirs have trilled, brass bands have blared out, folk dancers have cut pretty and colourful patterns, circus artists have tumbled and juggled. Some of the summer audiences have lasted over three hours.

Visiting Japanese, their cameras at the ready, are mystified by this display of Western religious culture. Pious Catholics have been known to be puzzled by John Paul's frank speaking on human sexuality. At the audience of 4 June, for example, they heard John Paul read out the following summary in English:

I am continuing today my talks on the first chapters of the book of Genesis. There we read that, after their disobedience, Adam and Eve felt shame at being naked and took to hiding their bodies from each other. There was a break in the original capacity of human beings to be in communion with each other. Gone was the simplicity and purity of the original experience, which enabled them to communicate themselves so fully.
Man and woman were intended to communicate, not just through the union by which husband and wife become one flesh, but in the communion of persons in which they were created to live. Their bodies were something underlying this communion. Their maleness and femaleness indicated clearly the significance of their bodies for full communion of persons. But after their disobedience, their sexuality

Each week throughout the summer the crowds gathered . . .

became an obstacle in the personal relationship between man and woman.
Their shame was a sign of their separation from the love that they were created to share, the love that is of the Father. Instead they came under the influence of concupiscence.
Next week, please God, I shall continue these considerations.

He did.

The disconcerting thing about these mini-lectures—they come complete with learned footnotes—is not their plain speaking about human sexuality. It is their abstract air and their unintelligibility in isolation. They presuppose that one has followed the whole series and remembered what was said the previous week. But most pilgrims come only to one audience and consequently they sometimes feel baffled or let down. The explanation for this curious behaviour on the part of the Pope is that he already had a book ready in draft form. He knows that as Pope he is not allowed to publish a book but that he can, and indeed must, publish his speeches. So he reads out chunks of the book to his Wednesday audiences. It is not the best instance of good communications. It is in the moments of informality on Wednesdays that John Paul is at his best. 'Once I used to climb mountains,' he said on one occasion. 'Now all I have to climb is this podium.'

Having said that, it should be added that the Wednesday lectures have a long-term value insofar as they represent a new kind of pontifical language on sexuality. John Paul is deliberately trying to develop something that has been lacking: a theology of the body. The neo-Platonic tendency to regard the soul as the prisoner of its temporary lodging, the body, has been definitively abandoned. The body shares in the goodness of creation. But this also means that the man/woman contrast is heavily stressed in John Paul's thinking. He could say with Freud that sexuality is destiny. Maleness and femaleness are fundamental categories, and they are not interchangeable. It is no doubt thoughts like these that are at the root of his opposition to homosexuality and the ordination of women: they offend against the sexual specialisation implanted in nature. But I doubt if many of his hearers at the Wednesday audiences are aware of such thinking—or could understand it if they were.

. . . in St Peter's Square to hear the Pope speak.

The other regular time for meeting the people is at the *Angelus* (or the *Regina Coeli* in Eastertide) at noon on Sunday mornings. The Pope delivers a ten-minute homily from his window and then greets the crowd and speaks more informally for another ten minutes. After the blessing he wishes them a 'Good Sunday' and departs. These occasions can be used for dramatic announcements. It was on Sunday morning, 19 November, that John Paul revealed that he would be going to Turkey within twelve days: till then his press office had been steadfastly denying that any such visit was contemplated. On another occasion he made a moving plea for the release of Annabel Schild, the daughter of a British engineer (of German origin) who was being held to ransom by Sardinian bandits. The girl was released, badly shaken but unhurt.

The liturgy provides another chance to see the Pope. Apart from Christmas and Easter, John Paul has frequently said Mass in St Peter's on special occasions. One of his most moving homilies was on the death of Vittorio Bachelet, a judge and former leader of Catholic Action in Italy, who was murdered by the Red Brigades. John Paul has in fact administered all the sacraments

One of the 45 priests ordained at the Easter Vigil.

Solemn Mass in St Peter's on Maundy Thursday.

that a bishop can. At the Easter Vigil he baptized twenty-four adults drawn from all over the world. On 15 June he ordained forty-five new priests. And on the morning of Good Friday astonished penitents found him in a confessional box in St Peter's. His attitude is best summed up in a remark he made to French young people in Parc des Princes on the evening of 1 July: 'I've been Pope for nearly two years, a bishop for over twenty years, but for me the most important thing is still the fact that I am a priest.' Becoming Pope enabled him to extend his priesthood to the whole world.

Without leaving Vatican territory, then, John Paul has accomplished what most people would be content to regard as a full year's work. Of course he has used the Vatican as the springboard for his worldwide mission. But before we can come to that, we will have to consider him as Bishop of Rome and Primate of Italy.

3

Rome needs a Bishop

Urbi et orbi, the Easter blessing of Rome and the world.

John Paul II has taken his duties as Bishop of Rome very seriously. He has done this for theological and ecumenical reasons. For he knows that 'Bishop of Rome' is the foundation of all his grander titles. He proposes to be a local bishop, just as he was in Cracow. Of course this is literally impossible. But the word 'impossible' is not in John Paul's Polish vocabulary.

There is also a practical reason for taking seriously the task of Bishop of Rome: pastoral work in Rome has been neglected for centuries. As long as the popes were at the same time temporal sovereigns of the Papal States (till 1870) there was a contradiction, or at best a conflict, between the role of ruler, with his censors, security police and executioners, and that of pastor. After 1870 matters were not improved, for the popes stayed sulking in the Vatican and did not recognize the new Italian state. Even after the quarrel had been resolved by the Lateran Treaty, signed with Mussolini in 1929, popes rarely left the Vatican. Paul VI felt deeply about the city and its problems. He emerged occasionally. He also met the clergy of Rome as a body, but they had to come to the Vatican to see him, and he would be flanked by the Cardinal Secretary of State and curial cardinals. That did not make for a spontaneous or a fraternal encounter.

Appropriate transport from the Vatican to Mass with Rome's railway workers in October.

Against this background, one can begin to appreciate the originality of John Paul II. He has set about a systematic visitation of all the 292 parishes of Rome, and in the course of the year has been to over twenty of them, always on Sunday evenings. These visits are the most 'visible' sign of his commitment to the diocese. I will come back to them in a moment.

The traditional washing of the feet during the Maundy Thursday liturgy.

More important for the long-term future was his visit to the Lateran Palace on 21 February. The church of St John Lateran is the home of the diocese of Rome. It is the Pope's cathedral church. Popes lived off and on in the Lateran Palace until 1347. When John Paul went there he was flanked not by Vatican officials but by Cardinal Ugo Poletti and the auxiliary bishops who look after the Rome diocese on the Pope's behalf. 'I felt I was present', said one of the participants, 'at a truly theological event.' The meeting lasted for over three hours, and John Paul listened more than he spoke. He admitted his ignorance ('this diocese was almost unknown to me') and stressed his readiness to learn. What he learned was not good news. The problems of Rome were analysed with devastating precision by members of the Council of Priests.

In conventional rhetoric Rome is 'the mother and head of all Churches'. But this does not mean that it is exemplary—on the contrary. There is very little sense of cohesion in the diocese of Rome. It has only 1,153 priests engaged in pastoral work for a population of over three million. Hardly any of them are Roman-born. Rome does not supply its own priestly needs. Nor is this new. Here is a sample of the ordination figures for the Rome diocese in this century: 1900, 10; 1925, 2; 1950, 12; 1975, 6; 1978, 7. As a result, over half of the priests working in the Rome diocese belong to religious orders; of the rest, many are volunteers from other Italian dioceses who return home after doing their Roman stint. In these conditions it is difficult to work out a coherent pastoral strategy.

The truth is that Rome got out of hand while no one was looking. The population has grown tenfold in a hundred years. Once it was pastorally manageable; now it is not. Strange as it may seem, there are not enough churches in Rome, and seventy of the parishes lack a proper church building. The visitor gets the impression, on the contrary, that there are churches at every corner of Rome; but they are in the 'historic centre', not where the people are.

The effects of pastoral neglect can be traced in the decline of religious practice. In 1960, 89 per cent of the babies born in Rome were baptized; by 1977 the figure had slumped to 81 per cent. More significant still, in 1963, 96.8 per cent of the marriages in Rome were celebrated in church; by 1978 the figure had fallen dramatically to 73.9 per cent. More than a quarter of Romans, in short, now content themselves with a civil marriage (if they bother to get married at all). John Paul listened to these statistics of decline, his head tilted to one side, his customary jaunty optimism gone.

Obviously not all these problems can be tackled, still less resolved, at once. Nor is the personal charisma of John Paul II in itself enough to reverse a historical process. But he has made a start. On the feast of Christ the King, 25 November 1979, the involved laity of the diocese were summoned to St Peter's for a special Mass celebrated by John Paul. Briefed by Cardinal Poletti and his team, he outlined the many social problems which Rome has to face: insecurity about jobs, housing and education; the disarray of new arrivals from rural areas; the lack of communication between families living in vast blocks of flats; organised crime, especially drug rackets; senseless violence and political terrorism. The indictment was formidable. Most of the industrialised world's problems are on the Pope's doorstep.

In his visits to the parishes, John Paul has sought to bring the Gospel to bear on these problems. Sunday by Sunday he has tried to rekindle the sense of community and mutual service. He has visited not only the parish churches but the hospitals, the hostels for drug addicts, the prisons for young offenders. He has gone to ancient city parishes like the church of the Holy Apostles, which has only eight hundred parishioners, and gigantic suburban parishes with over forty thousand people.

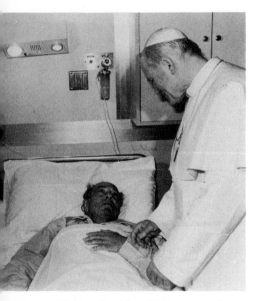

Visiting the sick at Christmas – at the Santo Spirito hospital in Rome.

But the story is not one of unrelieved gloom. One parish visitation had a special interest. On Sunday 18 May John Paul went to the parish dedicated to the Sacred Heart of Christ the King (a mouthful that is very revealing about the theology of the period). Coincidence number one was that 18 May happened to be John Paul's sixtieth birthday. Coincidence number two was that the foundation stone of the church had been laid on 18 May 1920, the very day on which the Pope was born in Wadowice. So he was able to exploit the joke that 'this church and I are contemporaries'. To mark the occasion the parish presented him with a mammoth birthday-cake, fashioned by a local pastry-cook with much volunteer help. On a base of three steps

The very big birthday cake.

rose the cake model of the parish church. A trembling child made a little speech. 'Our cake is very big', he said nervously, 'but our affection for you is even bigger.'

John Paul replied that the cake presented him with 'a very grave problem', given that there were so many hungry people in the world. He would only accept this gift, provided all the children of the parish helped him to eat it up. But there was another condition: as they ate, they must think of the children all around the world who still went hungry. Then he blew out the single candle, and the cake was cut up.

No one would seriously claim that this instance of papal pedagogy made a major contribution towards solving the intractable problems of the diocese of Rome. But the idea of the Church as one big, sharing party is not so absurd, and is well adapted to the Roman mentality. And the incident shows that John Paul is now thoroughly at home and accepted by the Romans. They have adopted him as one of their own. That is the first condition of being an effective Bishop of Rome. It makes a start. It cannot be said of John Paul that he won the away matches but lost those at home.

4 'My Second Homeland'

A visitation to the parish of St Martin, Rome.

Compared with the extensive coverage given to the Pope's international journeys, his travels within Italy aroused scant interest elsewhere. No doubt this was because it was assumed that popes must be expected to travel freely in the country which surrounds the Vatican City State. But this principle is far from obvious, and in fact since 1870 popes have on the whole preferred to stay inside the Vatican. John XXIII made the first timid breach in this tradition. He went by train to Assisi and Loreto, and his choice of pilgrimage centres made it clear that he was sticking firmly to his religious role and not in any way reviving the claims of the former Papal States. Protocol demanded this kind of scrupulous discretion.

It proved easier for the first non-Italian Pope for 455 years to go beyond protocol and to travel into the (technically) foreign Republic of Italy. It helps that he has struck up an extremely good relationship with Sandro Pertini, the diminutive and grandfatherly socialist who is President. Nor does he have the kind of contact with the leading Christian Democrats that both John XXIII and Paul VI had. So the 'Italian factor', by which is meant the habit of judging international questions in the light of Italian needs, weighs down upon him less than on any previous modern pope. The result is that he appears in Italy as a 'spiritual leader' who wants to bring to this traditionally Catholic but now highly secularised country the joy and hope of the Gospel. A further mark in his favour is that he has referred to Italy as 'my second homeland': he now speaks the language effectively and can engage in impromptu dialogue with the crowds.

And crowds there certainly were for his two main sorties, on 21 October to Naples and on 13 April to Turin. Naples is the capital of the *mezzogiorno*, the troubled south, where the *per capita* income is half that of the prosperous north, and where unemployment, under-employment and child-employment are endemic. In fact the Pope's long day in the south began at the Marian shrine of Pompei. In his homily there, and for the first time, John Paul seemed to be answering objections about the show-business aspect of his journeys. It was only two weeks after returning from his spectacular United States visit. He said that he had prepared for that transatlantic journey 'on his knees' and that the essence of his ministry was 'to open the ways of the Holy Spirit'. 'All the rest', he concluded, brushing aside his critics, 'is a display that humanly speaking could be considered superficial.' The crowd was on his side. People roared their approval.

In Naples itself that same afternoon the mood was one of high festival. The city may be impoverished but it can put on a good show. The sky was limpid and blue. Naples forgot its troubles and celebrated the presence of John Paul—the first Pope to visit the city since 1870. A polyphonic choir launched what must be called the anthem of Naples, *O Sole Mio*, and an estimated half a million people joined in. Enzo Mangia, writing in *Osservatore Romano*, was moved to remark: 'The Neapolitans saw in the

Vicar of Christ their Sun, the light that recreates inner order . . .
Thus the profane was transformed into the sacred, reversing the
secularising trends of the age' (23–24 October 1979). Forsooth!
That is the kind of thing that gives the Vatican newspaper a bad
name. When John Paul could eventually make himself heard he
delivered an address on the theme of justice and charity. They
are not in opposition: 'Charity, the first duty of every Christian,
does not make justice superfluous; and justice, the cardinal
virtue, calls for and is filled out by charity.' These were
sentiments which the many Communist voters in the crowd
could applaud.

Crowds in Turin during the Pope's
visit.

Turin has almost as many problems as Naples, though of a
different kind. Dominated by the Fiat car industry, now
undergoing a recession, it has been a city of sharp social
conflicts and the headquarters of terrorism. On 13 April, 700,000
people saw John Paul, which is half the population of Turin and
twice its average Sunday Mass attendance. Once again there
was a festival. It was as though John Paul managed to create a
no-man's-land, a truce area, in which everyone could hope
again. The kiss of peace in the vast square outside the cathedral
was for many the most moving part of the whole visit. There
were none of the reluctant finger-tip handshakes that
Anglo-Saxons go in for, but whole-hearted embraces for anyone
within range.

The local 'basic Christian communities' tried to protest against
the visit on the grounds that it would reinforce the unjust *status
quo*. But their voices and banners were lost in the crowd. If they
listened, they would have heard John Paul make an
even-handed criticism of both capitalism and communism. He
trod a careful path between unrestricted capitalism, with its
inhuman work rhythms, its tendency to disrupt family ties and
its capacity to bewilder the young, and communism which, by
declaring God dead, makes orphans of us all. He seemed to be
saying that the Church was outside and above this conflict, and
that it possessed in its social teaching the key to the
transformation of society. This came out in the way he
denounced the two intellectual forces that have shaped the
modern world, liberalism and Marxism:

There is on the one hand the rationalist, scientistic, Enlightenment approach of the secular so-called 'liberalism' of Western nations, which carries with it the radical denial of Christianity; and on the other hand the ideology and praxis of atheistic 'Marxism' whose materialistic principles are taken to their most extreme consequences in various forms of contemporary terrorism.

That, at least, was the version of the address as written, and very largely as reported by corner-cutting journalists. But in the address as actually delivered, John Paul omitted the last clause, and did not make an explicit link between Marxism and terrorism. Was this for reasons of prudence? Or had he been advised at the last moment that the Italian Communists, eager for respectability and office, have been among the most resolute opponents of terrorism? Whatever the answer, the curious result was that the condemnation of 'liberalism' seemed sharper than that of 'Marxism'.

There was another, less fraught, journey within Italy. On 23 March John Paul went to Norcia where St Benedict was born approximately 1,500 years ago. Norcia is a small hill town difficult of access and defended by stout walls. John Paul developed the theme of Benedict as peacemaker and architect of civilisation. 'Nothing constructive is achieved by violence,' he told the young people. 'We have to build the civilisation of love.' The cheers echoed round the ancient walls. In his homily he dwelt on the Benedictine motto, *laborare est orare*, to work is to pray, and found it highly relevant in the modern world which needs to discover the right balance between contemplation and action. But the visit to Norcia was not all speech-making. John Paul gave it a pastoral dimension by meeting the victims of an earthquake in their new prefabricated homes.

With the people of Norcia in March.

Early autumn was a particularly busy time. John Paul went to Aquila, Siena and Otranto. Otranto, with its castle jutting out into the Adriatic, is the easternmost point of Italy. From there many of the crusaders set sail. And there, five hundred years ago, 800 Christians were frog-marched up the Hill of Minerva and beheaded by the Turks. John Paul spoke from the very place where they were slaughtered. But he did not dwell on the past and held out a hand of friendship to Islam. He preferred to speak of 'the martyrs of our own age who are often unknown and yet not so far distant from us'. With a sweeping gesture he indicated that he was thinking of Albania, only seventy kilometres away across the Adriatic, where the Church has been all but destroyed. That was on 5 October.

But it was the visit to Siena two weeks earlier (21 September) that proved to be the most controversial of all John Paul's Italian journeys. He was there ostensibly to celebrate the 600th anniversary of the death of St Catherine, who, with St Francis, is the patron of Italy. He dealt with her adequately enough. But his main theme was 'the right to life'. 'The Church judges no one,' he cried, his voice rising to a dramatic crescendo, 'but it cannot fail to bear witness to the truth: every attack on the child in its mother's womb is a great blow to conscience. It is a great disgrace. It is a great sorrow.' Forty thousand people made it clear that they agreed with this anti-abortion statement.

It was the context that made it controversial. Abortion has been legal in Italy since 18 May 1978. Since then, there have been 400,000 abortions, an average of 600 a day. Earlier in 1980 the Radical Party gathered enough signatures to demand a referendum designed to 'liberalize' the law on abortion still further. The Pro-life movement responded by collecting signatures for a referendum of its own. On the Sundays just before the Siena visit, notaries were present outside parish churches to record the signatures and check that there was no doubling up. If half-a-million Italian citizens sign a petition, then according to law there must be a referendum.

So the Pope's words were interpreted by the Radical and Socialist Parties as the opening of a crusade. His intervention was said to be 'a flagrant interference in the internal affairs of the Republic of Italy'. The leader of the Socialists, Bettino Craxi, said in Parliament that John Paul II was 'a foreigner who did not understand the Italian constitution'. The bishops replied indignantly that this was an insulting charge and that the Pope had a perfect right and duty to proclaim moral principles whenever and wherever he spoke. John Paul's own view was simply that he should not be less free to speak his mind in Italy than he had been in Poland. But there is a real threat of a constitutional crisis ahead, which could affect the much-delayed revision of the Concordat between the Holy See and Italy.

A private moment in a public place.

Gradually, then, what might be called John Paul's Italian strategy began to emerge. He will be courteous to the civil authorities but not have a special relationship with the Christian Democratic Party. His appeal is directly to the ordinary people of Italy. His idea is to make Italy something that it never really was, despite centuries of tradition: a Christian nation. In Turin, home of the *Risorgimento*, he never once mentioned Camillo Cavour, the architect of Italian unity in the nineteenth century. Neither John XXIII nor Paul VI could have gone to Turin without reconciling themselves with the history of their own country.

The Polish Pope has a somewhat different map of his second homeland. He can be more easily permitted the dream of an alternative Italy, a land of shrines to the Madonna, of saints like Benedict, Catherine of Siena and Don John Bosco, of the Holy Shroud of Turin. There is enough weariness and disillusionment with lack-lustre politicians in the air for this dream to seem plausible.

On a more administrative level, the surprise announcement in December that Fr Carlo Martini, a fifty-three year old Jesuit, was to become the next Archbishop of the ancient and prestigious see of Milan, was further evidence of the new approach to Italian problems. By naming Martini, John Paul served notice that he would set aside the Italian ecclesiastical career structure, stiffen the intellectual calibre of the bench of bishops, and prefer 'spirituality' to good contacts with the Christian Democrats. Given time, this will change the Italian Church and with it the nation.

5

A Summit of Eminences

The announcement that there would be a meeting of cardinals in the Vatican from 5 to 9 November 1979 was another of John Paul's surprises. Though the college of cardinals is supposed to advise the Pope, it had not met in the last four hundred years except on the death of a pope, when its sole task was to elect a new one. The two conclaves of 1978, in August and then again unexpectedly in October, had given the cardinals a unique chance to work together and to get to know each other better. Immediately after his election, John Paul had spoken of 'developing new forms of collegiality'. The meeting of cardinals—the proper term, consistory, was sedulously avoided—was an example of what he had in mind.

So the fact that this meeting happened at all was more important than what it discussed. In any case its proceedings were confidential, and only a very vague and general statement was issued at the end. There were three topics on the agenda: the reform of the Roman Curia, the Church and culture, and the present financial state of the Holy See.

The Roman Curia is the Pope's bureaucracy. It is divided into a number of departments called Congregations or, for those founded since Vatican II, Secretariats, Councils or Commissions. They act very much as ministries do in a government administration. There is input and output: they receive information and prepare documents and decisions. In 1961 the Roman Curia had 1,322 members; by 1978 it had swollen to 3,146. This expansion, made necessary by the need to implement the decisions of Vatican II, had contributed to the financial problem. Collegiality is costly: it means lots of travel.

Pope Paul VI had an insider's knowledge of the strengths and weaknesses of the Curia. He had tried to reform it by streamlining it and bringing everything under the co-ordinating control of the Secretariat of State. John Paul II has so far not revealed his plans for the Curia. Though he has been solicitous about individuals, he has not shown great interest in its arcane operations. But the significant thing is that he did not ask the Curia to reform itself, as Paul VI trustfully had done; as an outsider who had never worked in the Curia, he has invited the college of cardinals to make proposals for its reform.

Opening up the Vatican's secrets? The opening session of the meeting of cardinals, 5 November 1979.

The cardinals, too, are for the most part outsiders. They have the objections to the Curia that people have to bureaucracy generally: time-consuming delay, occasional arrogance, and a tendency to usurp the functions of diocesan bishops. The cardinals could make suggestions in writing up to three months after the conclusion of their meeting. So far nothing has been divulged about their proposals. But the result of the meeting is that the Pope can do what he likes with the Curia, which is at his service and at the service of the universal Church.

An understandably affectionate embrace from elder statesman to new president: Cardinal Wyszynski and Pope John Paul.

The second theme of the meeting, the Church and culture, sounds like an invitation to waffle and windiness. Yet it corresponds to a concern very close to the heart of John Paul. His aim is to close the gap, or at least to reduce the opposition, between secular and Christian culture, science and faith. His Polish background makes him sensitive to the way the State in Communist countries exploits 'culture' to impose its own ideology so that alternative cultural traditions are made to appear 'reactionary' and out of date. But what is to be done? One suggestion is that there may be founded a Pontifical Academy of the Human Sciences (sociology, psychology, etc.) to meet the contemporary challenge to faith which no longer comes from the physical sciences or biology.

A further insight into the thinking of John Paul II was given on 10 November, the day after the meeting of cardinals concluded. He was addressing the Pontifical Academy of Sciences, founded in 1922. Its members are distinguished scientists who do not have to be Catholics or even believers. Though the gathering was ostensibly devoted to celebrating the hundredth anniversary of the birth of Albert Einstein, John Paul seized the opportunity virtually to re-habilitate Galileo (who in 1633 had been forced to deny that the earth went round the sun). 'The greatness of Galileo is recognized by all', he said, 'but we cannot deny that he suffered greatly at the hands of Church bodies.' Obviously the reconciliation of science and faith is a long-term programme lacking instant, reach-me-down solutions. But John Paul showed his determination that questions of culture should not be overlooked in the Curia by making the French Cardinal Gabriel-Marie Garrone responsible for this area.

It was the remaining topic on the agenda that attracted most interest in the media: the mystery of Vatican finances. Is the Vatican inappropriately rich or on the verge of bankruptcy? It is almost impossible to answer this question, given the overlapping bodies involved, the array of fluctuating currencies that have to be considered, and the distinctions that have to be made. If the contents of the Vatican museums could be sold off or if St Peter's could be torn down and replaced by luxury flats, then clearly the Vatican would be very rich. But none of these assets are seriously realisable.

In his final address to the college of cardinals John Paul spoke of the 'fables and myths' surrounding the vast wealth of the Vatican. A balance-sheet has never been made public. There is some evidence that John Paul was hoping to be able to publish one, but that he met with resistance among his financial advisers. One statistic, however, was produced, and for the first time. The deficit forecast for the year 1979 was just over 20 million dollars, and worse was anticipated for the year 1980.

This did not mean that the Vatican was going broke, since the deficit was covered 'thanks to the voluntary offerings coming from the Catholic world, particularly from Peter's Pence' (an annual collection held in some countries). In any case, the profits made by the investments of the Vatican bank—known as the Institute for the Works of Religion—were not included in this accounting. Its president, Archbishop Paul Marcinkus, from Cicero, Illinois, is also the tough-looking bodyguard one sees alongside the Pope during his travels.

But the single statistic revealed was enough to place an axe over the Roman Curia. There will have to be cuts. It also explained John Paul's appeal to the cardinals that Churches that were 'rich and free' should come to the aid of those that were neither rich nor free. There was an urgent need, he said for 'solidarity and social charity'. Some observers took this to mean that there would be some kind of tax on the wealthy Churches of the West in order to provide support for those of Eastern Europe and the third world. But so far nothing further has been heard of this suggestion.

It would be easier to evaluate the meeting of cardinals if we knew what they actually said to each other. But we don't. Certainly, to judge by his opening address, John Paul invited them to approve the main lines of his pontificate: the implementation of Vatican II, but without hasty and erroneous interpretations of that Council. Armed with the approval or at least the acquiescence of the college of cardinals, John Paul could then proceed with his dialogue with the Orthodox Churches and to deal more confidently with 'dissident' theologians and with the Dutch Church. That, anyway, is what he did next. The first consultation with the cardinals was in the nature of a trial run. No doubt there will be others.

6 *Eastern Approaches*

The Pope being greeted on arrival at Ankara by President Fahri Koroturk.

Pope John Paul's fourth international journey (coming after Mexico, Poland, Ireland and the United States) was the most bizarre to date. There were no pope-mobiles, babies to be blessed, ticker-tape parades, or cheering crowds. Instead there was silence, threats of assassination, and heavily armed soldiery. There is considerable evidence that the Turkish government was less than enthusiastic about the papal visit—understandably. It had just been shakily elected (it has since fallen), political assassinations were happening at an average of three a day, and the population of forty-five millions is predominantly Moslem. John Paul had described his previous journeys as 'pastoral' or 'apostolic'. Asked on the plane to qualify this journey, he prudently said that it was a 'fraternal visit'. Anything more than that would have been regarded as an insult by the sensitive Turks.

The Pope's welcome was as cool as the wind blowing down from the Anatolian Mountains. He was a 'visiting head of state'.

The now-traditional kissing of the ground non-plussing the Pope's Turkish hosts.

There were no speeches at the airport, or at the tomb of Ataturk, the founder of modern Turkey. Indeed, it was not until the second day of his journey, Thursday 29 November, that John Paul was able to speak in public at all, and even then it was to a very restricted public. He preached in the chapel of the Italian Embassy in Ankara. He let himself be guided by historical memories. This was a land very closely connected with the origins of Christianity. Peter and Paul had been here; Galatia and Cappadocia (mentioned in the First Epistle of Peter) were nearby. There was, claimed John Paul, an analogy between then and now. Christians were in a minority: they had a duty to the civil authorities. 'Act as free men,' he quoted, 'not as men who use liberty as a cloak of malice' (1 Peter 2.16). It was an elegant tribute to the Turkish government.

Turkey has a common frontier with Iran. This gave added importance to John Paul's homily in which he exhorted Christians and Moslems to seek common ground. Though his envoys in Iran had been constantly rebuffed, he said that he admired 'the spiritual heritage of Islam, its ability to offer to all and especially to young people a sense of direction in their life, to fill the vacuum of materialism and to provide a basis for social and legal organisation'. But the Pope did not really go to Turkey to open up a new phase in Christian-Moslem relations.

A warmer manner of greeting for the Archbishop of Constantinople, 'the new Rome', from the Bishop of (old?) Rome.

The point of his journey became clear the next day when he flew to Istanbul—the Turks do not like it to be called Constantinople—to meet Patriarch Dimitrios I whose full title, from the fifth century, is 'Archbishop of Constantinople, the new Rome, and Ecumenical Patriarch'. The Patriarch is not the 'Pope' of the East, for no such office exists. He has no real authority over the other autocephalous (independently-ruled) Orthodox Churches. But he is the first in seniority, has great

Gregorian Armenian Patriarch Schnork Kalutsyan greets Pope John Paul.

symbolic importance and has convenor's rights. When authorized by the thirteen Orthodox Churches, he can act as their go-between. This is precisely what happened during the visit.

The ground had been painstakingly prepared by Paul VI and Patriarch Athenagoras. Pope and Patriarch embraced each other, in Jerusalem, as brother to brother. On 7 December 1965, the day before the Second Vatican Council ended, the mutual excommunications of 1054 and subsequent years were rescinded in solemn ceremonies in St Peter's, Rome, and at the Orthodox Cathedral of St George in Constantinople. But now it was time to move to a new stage of dialogue. The dialogue of charity was to be carried further forwards: it was to be completed by the 'dialogue of truth', a full theological discussion in which it was hoped that the remaining differences could be overcome so that 'full and perfect communion' might be realised.

The Orthodox have a keen sense of symbolic events and symbolic gifts. They are not regarded as 'empty gestures' and can be more eloquent than laborious words. Patriarch Dimitrios presented John Paul with a stole: that meant he was recognizing him as a true priest. John Paul's gift was trundled up the aisle of the cathedral of St George in a wooden packing-case. The Moslem troops looked on indifferently. When opened, the packing-case revealed a copy of the picture of Our Lady of Czestochowa from Poland. This was more than just a nice thought. It was a reminder that there are historical links between Poland and Constantinople. The picture of Our Lady is an icon, and it arrived mysteriously from somewhere in the East in the fifteenth century. Moreover, John Paul alluded to the fact that the mission of SS. Cyril and Methodius, which set out from Constantinople in the ninth century to convert the Slav peoples, actually reached and baptized the Vislani tribe living in the southern part of Poland. So John Paul draws the conclusion that as a Polish pope he has a special role to play in the dialogue between East and West, between Catholicism and Orthodoxy. The Poles live on the crossroads: they are Latin by tradition but Slav by race.

This helps to explain why, in ecumenical matters, John Paul gives priority to union with the Orthodox Churches, rather than closer ties with the Churches which emerged from the Reformation. Unity between Catholics and the Orthodox, he said, 'would be a fundamental and decisive step in the progress of the entire ecumenical movement. Our division has perhaps not been without influence on later divisions.' To understand this, one has to recall a theory that was advanced by Fr Yves-Marie Congar O.P. and others in the 1950s: if the schism between East and West had not tragically occurred, then maybe the Reformation would have been unnecessary. The West would not have been able to impose its Roman, juridical style on everyone, and there would have been an acceptance of differences as an enrichment rather than as grounds for division.

There is much that Catholics and Orthodox have in common: high sacramental doctrine, Christology and the Trinity, a reverence for monasticism, devotion to Mary (John Paul went to

An ecumenical service in an unmistakably Orthodox setting.

Ephesus to emphasise this point). The outstanding differences concern the post-division councils which have been held by the Roman Catholic Church without the participation of the Orthodox. Particularly craggy is the First Vatican Council (1869–70) which defined papal infallibility and the Pope's 'universal jurisdiction'.

This is something that the Orthodox cannot swallow. So it was particularly interesting to note the way John Paul talked about his own office in Constantinople. He talked in 'Greek' and non-juridical terms. He described Peter, younger brother of Andrew (patron of the Church of Constantinople), as 'the chorus leader of the apostles'—a phrase used in the Orthodox liturgical texts. His own mission was stated in the mildest form as that of 'ensuring the harmony of apostolic teaching'. 'Harmony' is another Greek term that does not portend anything sinister. He said that Peter, 'as a brother among brothers,' was entrusted 'with the task of confirming the apostles in faith'. This moderate statement of 'Roman claims' was sweet music to Orthodox ears.

It allowed the 'theological dialogue' to proceed, and in fact the Roman Catholic/Orthodox Joint Dialogue Committee held its first meeting on the islands of Patmos and Rhodes from 29 May to 4 June 1980. It was a somewhat unwieldy body with thirty members from each side. It proposed an agenda for future work, to be dealt with in a number of sub-committees. It expressed the hope 'that the re-establishment of the full communion of our churches will contribute to the reconciliation of mankind and to the peace of the world of which the Church is the sign and divine instrument according to the will of God.' The most remarkable thing about this dialogue is that the Orthodox Churches were able to agree among themselves.

Hopes of union have been raised before, notably in 1439 when the Council of Florence reached an agreement but could not make it stick. The Committee is lucid about the difficulties, and anxious to avoid the 'mistakes' of the Council of Florence. For one thing, Church leaders are to be involved from the outset, so will not be taken by surprise. Again, no one is this time in any hurry, so there will be time for the psychological preparation of the people on both sides. Finally, and most crucial of all, the dialogue will start from points of agreement rather than from points of divergence.

John Paul commented on the importance of his visit to Turkey at the audience of 5 December 1980. He made most of the points already made here. He concluded with the rather cryptic remark: 'I was asked by one of the journalists on the plane for my "impressions" of the journey, and I said that it was a very difficult question to answer. It really is difficult. We are in another dimension. . . . But we are serving the great cause of the coming of the Lord.'

The Pope may feel that he is in another dimension. But anyone who wishes to understand his pontificate will have to grasp that he is playing for very high stakes indeed. Union with the Orthodox would mean a significant change in the balance of forces in Eastern Europe. The biggest Orthodox Church by far is the Russian Orthodox Church. Union with it could lead to a destabilisation of the Communist regime not by any pressure from the outside but simply because it would no longer correspond to what the people of the Soviet Union felt.

John Paul is very close to the vision of Solzhenitsyn. This is the key to his pontificate. It marks a shift to the East. It is perilous and could fail. But if it fails, it will be a magnificent, very Polish failure. Though reluctant to share his 'impressions' of his journey to Turkey, John Paul did say to one of the journalists on his return flight that he would be ready to go to Moscow, the 'third Rome'.

7 *Theologians in Hot Water*

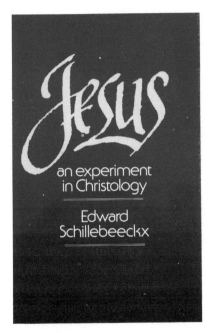

Book and author (1)

The most controversial episode in the pontificate so far came just before Christmas. A Flemish Dominican, Eduard Schillebeeckx, and a Swiss professor, Hans Küng, found themselves at odds with the Congregation for the Doctrine of Faith. Formerly known as the Holy Office and with historical links with the Inquisition, this Congregation is the watchdog of orthodoxy and sound doctrine. It had been 'reformed' by Paul VI in 1967 and 1971, but now it appeared to be reverting to type. Schillebeeckx was summoned to Rome for a 'colloquy' or conversation on his best-selling book, *Jesus, an Experiment in*

Christology (the original Dutch title, *Jesus, the Story of a Living Person,* was more accurate and less provocative). On the day his investigation was concluded, 15 December, the Congregation for the Doctrine of Faith produced a declaration which said that 'Professor Hans Küng could no longer be regarded as a Catholic

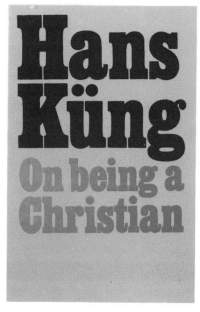

Book and author (2) . . .

theologian', and his mandate to teach as such was withdrawn. It was not released until four days later, by which time the German Bishops had published another declaration which gave further details, but added that Küng remained a priest and a Catholic. So he was relegated to a rather curious limbo in which he could be a Catholic theologian but not actually utter as one.

Protests had been building up long before Schillebeeckx reached Rome, first in Holland but then more widely in Britain and the United States. They were intensified when Küng was condemned. At issue was academic freedom, the future of the ecumenical movement, and a conflict of views about precisely how a theologian's work should be related to the *magisterium* or teaching authority of the Church.

Those who sought to defend Schillebeeckx and Küng did not dispute that a theologian has pastoral responsibility or that he should respect the tradition which nourished him. But they also held that a theologian had the right and duty to restate that tradition so as to make it intelligible for the people of today who found it difficult to grasp concepts hammered out in the theological controversies of the fourth and fifth centuries. They

. . . v. the teaching authority of Rome.

had a good point when they argued that both Schillebeeckx's book on Jesus and Hans Küng's *On Being a Christian* had helped many ordinary people to understand better their Christian faith. Neither of them had the ambition or the outlook of an heresiarch.

Their defenders further claimed that even if theologians did go astray, the right people to deal with them were their professional colleagues. Fellow-theologians could point out mistakes, faulty reasoning, and illegitimate jumps. Hans Küng, for example, had not been allowed by his fellow scholars to get away with his apparently undermining remarks on the doctrine of infallibility. Heavy-handed interventions of authority, said the defence, could only make things worse: for they implied that theologians were not free to ask fundamental questions and were merely part of the conveyor-belt of the *magisterium*.

The Congregation for the Doctrine of Faith and Pope John Paul himself had a different approach to the problem. The Congregation conceded (or at least asserted) the academic freedom of theologians, but only within the strictest of limits laid down by the teaching authority of the Church. But it was more concerned with the ordinary faithful than with the fate of theologians. The faithful, said the declaration on Küng, 'have the sacred right to receive the Word of God uncontaminated, and so they expect that vigilant care should be exercised to keep the threat of error far from them.' The suggestion, therefore, was that Schillebeeckx maybe and Küng certainly had offended against this principle and were causing grave disquiet and upset among the faithful. The intervention of the Vatican was a defence of popular religion against the dangerous speculations of theologians.

Attempts were sometimes made to absolve John Paul from the actions of the Congregation for the Doctrine of Faith. But this was sheer wishful thinking. John Paul has spoken about theology on a number of occasions (at greatest length to the International Theological Commission on 22 October) and he has always stressed the general principle that the theologian should be strictly subordinate to the Church's *magisterium*. His task is to defend and illustrate what it proposes. Literal fidelity is required of him. His research may well reveal new aspects of old truths, but no appeal to 'historical context' can rob defined dogmas of their value and relevance for today. So the room for manoeuvre is small. John Paul repeated these ideas at the Gregorian University on the evening of 15 December, the very day on which Schillebeeckx's hearing was concluded and the Küng condemnation signed. Three coincidences are too much for mere chance.

In any case, although John Paul has not spoken directly on the issues raised by Schillebeeckx, he has massively intervened on the matter of Küng. On 22 May he addressed a weighty letter to the German Bishops in which he commended them for their collaboration with the Congregation for the Doctrine of Faith. It was, he said, an instance of 'collegiality'. Not only that, but he entered into controversy with Küng on the precise point at issue: infallibility. It was 'a gift of Christ to the Church'. 'We must be very worried when this gift of Christ is cast into doubt.'

The reason why infallibility is so important is stated thus: 'When this essential basis of faith is weakened or destroyed, the most elementary truths of our faith begin to collapse.' It is highly unusual for a pope to intervene in so personal a way on a controverted theological question.

At the time of writing, the 'verdict' in the Schillebeeckx case is still awaited, though Schillebeeckx hopes to get off lightly (he has the invaluable support of Cardinal Jo Willebrands). Küng, meanwhile, after breathing threatening noises about legal proceedings, has tactfully withdrawn from the Catholic Faculty of Theology in the University of Tübingen, but continues to direct the Institute for Ecumenical Research there.

The public reaction to the two cases seems to have discouraged, for the time being, further theological trials. In January it became known that Fr Leonardo Boff, a Brazilian Franciscan, had been in correspondence with the Congregation for the Doctrine of Faith. His book, *Jesus Christ, Liberator*, was said to raise problems about Jesus' knowledge of his impending death. But Bishop Ivo Lorscheiter, President of the Brazilian Episcopal Conference, warded off this attack and pointed out that the Brazilian bishops had confidence in Boff's orthodoxy. This may have been only a temporary victory. In his speech to the Brazilian bishops at Fortaleza on 10 July, John Paul told them that the Roman Curia acted on his behalf and must be obeyed. He reminded them, 'The true theologian knows, by a supernatural instinct, that it belongs to the bishop to watch over his theological activity for the sake of the faith of the people of God.' So we have not heard the last of this matter.

8   *Manning the Dykes*

The Dutch bishops at the opening of the Synod.

The possibility of holding a special synod to deal with the problems of a particular Church was included in the Synod regulations drawn up by Paul VI. But he had never made use of this provision. So John Paul was innovating yet again when he summoned a Synod of the Dutch Church to begin in Rome on 14 January. A further surprise was that the Synod should be held inside the Vatican where the Dutch bishops were isolated from their people, out-numbered and out-voted by the curial participants, and where relatively strict secrecy could be enforced.

Officially the purpose of the Synod was to consider 'the pastoral work of the Church in the Netherlands in the present situation'. But there would have been no point in discussing this unless enough people believed that there was a crisis in Holland and that pastoral work there was on a wrong track. Officially the goal of the Synod was 'that the Church should reveal itself to be a *communio*'. This Latin term points to the spiritual reality of the Church and stresses the need for unity. The Dutch bishops had been notoriously disunited. While four out of the seven had strongly supported the 'progressive' line taken by their Church since the Council, two (Simonis of Rotterdam and Gijsen of

Cardinal Willebrands, leader of the Dutch bishops, at the Pope's right hand during the opening Mass.

Roermond) were opposed to it. In between, vainly striving to keep the peace, was Cardinal Jo Willebrands. So the Synod was called to deal with the crisis and to resolve these differences.

A blanket of secrecy descended upon the Synod once the preliminaries were over. The Vatican press bulletins invited one to crack a mysterious code, the prize of success being blandness and banality. John Paul explained the reason for secrecy to Dutch journalists at a General Audience: 'I am sure you will understand that the Church, like all families, at least on certain occasions, needs to have moments of exchange, discussion and decision which take place in intimacy and discretion, to enable the participants to be free and to respect people and situations.'

Left to right, perhaps uncharacteristically, Bishops Adriaan Simonis of Rotterdam, Hubertus Ernst of Breda and Johannes Bluyssen of 's-Hertogenbosch.

The Dutch journalists, used to open government, found this hard to follow; and the suggestion that the bishops formed a family from which the rest of the Church was excluded seemed positively offensive. Because of the secrecy, we cannot say for certain whether the progressive Dutch bishops caved in from the start or whether they put up stout resistance before finally collapsing. When they emerged from the Synod on 31 January they were in a euphoric mood and claimed to have rediscovered their lost *communio*. To a man they paid tribute to John Paul who had shared the work with them and been present much more than anyone had expected.

The Dutch bishops went home with a twenty-two page document containing an introduction, forty-six propositions, and an epilogue about how to implement the propositions. Their main effect was to reinforce the distinction between people and hierarchy, between the laity and the ordained ministry. These distinctions had been breaking down in Holland under the pressure of pastoral need. Now they were re-asserted.

Bishops were reminded that they were true 'teachers' of the faith, not merely spokesmen for what the faithful chanced to believe. 'Neither bishops nor priests are the *delegates* of the faithful,' says conclusion 3. Conversely, the laity were not to take on roles proper to the priest. In Holland before the Synod there were some 300 'pastoral workers', including married men and women, who were theologically trained and who acted as 'curates' in parishes. It was often they rather than the elderly priest who preached on Saturday evenings or Sunday mornings. The only thing they did not do (though there were rumours of exceptions) was to celebrate the Eucharist. The Dutch had justified this experiment on the grounds that there were simply not enough ordained priests, and that no new ones were coming forwards. The Synod ordered an investigation into the role of the 'pastoral workers'. It clearly regarded them with disfavour.

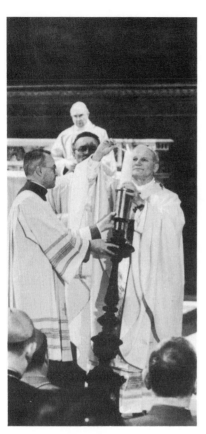

Lighting a candle of unity – or of hope.

It was difficult to escape the impression that the real purpose of the Synod was to bring the Dutch Church back into line and to put a stop to experimentation. There were warnings against liturgical improvisation, a too humanistic approach to catechetics, ecumenism seen as watering-down, and intercommunion. Former priests should cease to be employed in theological faculties and other Church posts. The media must be scrutinised (censored?) more vigilantly. Every effort must be made to encourage vocations to the priestly and religious life, and instead of an open university setting, students for the ministry must live either in regular seminaries or hostels where their spiritual formation could be supervised. Proposition 21 reports that the Dutch bishops were 'unanimous in their desire to follow faithfully the decisions of the popes and to maintain the rule of celibacy'. For some of them, this represented a *volte-face*.

Here one sees the weakness of the Dutch Synod. It looked like a clear-cut victory for John Paul and the Curia. The Dutch bishops were persuaded to abandon policies that most of them have been committed to for the last fifteen years. But there was no means of knowing whether the decisions made at the Synod could be carried out. A Church has to be convinced if it is to change. Some of the 'decisions' of the Synod are no more than pious wishes. Thus proposition 21 continues: 'The bishops hope to find a sufficient number of priests. But even if candidates are lacking, the members of the Synod profess their confidence in the Lord of the harvest who will send workers into the field.'

The real test of the Synod came when the bishops returned to Holland with their package of propositions. It would be untrue to say that they were greeted with enthusiasm as saviours of the Dutch Church. On the contrary it was widely felt that they had capitulated: this hardly enhanced their authority as 'true

Over to you – a sign of peace at the closing ceremony.

leaders' of their Church. So John Paul's victory may turn out to be a pyrrhic victory, with promising experiments destroyed or driven underground and mere lip-service being paid to the Synod.

Moreover, despite the initial euphoria, it has failed to unite the opposing factions of the Dutch hierarchy, as Bishop Gijsen made plain in the run-up to the September Synod of Bishops. When Cardinal Willebrands announced in August a 1981 session of the controversial Dutch National Catholic 'Consultation' (begun in 1978), he acknowledged that tensions might reemerge. All the signs are that they will.

Nevertheless, the Dutch Synod was an important event for the whole Church. It showed clearly what the limits of pluralism are as John Paul conceives them. It was an attempt at a restoration. One of the participants, Godefried Daneels, successor of Cardinal Suenens as Archbishop of Malines in Belgium, said that the Synod was 'an interpretation of Vatican II for the 1980s'. If that is true, Vatican II has been safely domesticated.

9 *The Ukrainian Succession*

Tucked away at the end of the Vatican news bulletin for 18 March was the laconic statement: 'To provide for the pastoral needs of the Ukrainian Catholic Church, John Paul II has summoned the Ukrainian bishops to a Synod which will begin in the Vatican on 24 March 1980.' A mere six days' notice of the Synod was given to the world at large. The secret had been astonishingly well-kept.

The reason for this belated announcement may have been to allow the Vatican delegation, which was then visiting the Soviet Union, to inform the Russian Orthodox in advance and to point out that the Synod posed no threat to them. For many years the Ukrainians had been a cause of friction between Rome and the Moscow Patriarchate. History provided the explanation: in 1948 the Russian Orthodox Church had hailed the destruction of the Ukrainian Catholic Church—legally, it had ceased to exist—as a great victory: and Ukrainians in exile felt resentful that the Vatican should be dealing with their oppressors.

Cardinal Josef Slipyi, the 88-year-old Major Archbishop of the Ukrainians, whose release from a Siberian labour camp had been negotiated by John XXIII in 1963, embodied the aggrieved feelings of the exiles. He asserted his independence of the Vatican by calling Synods of his own. He claimed the right to the title of Patriarch which Paul VI steadfastly refused on theological and juridical grounds. The result was that the 823,000 Ukrainian Catholics, mostly living in the United States or Canada, were split into pro- and anti-Patriarchate factions. This was the 'pastoral need' for which the Roman Synod had to provide.

John Paul stepped into this ecclesiastical minefield with great deftness. He has the advantage of speaking Ukrainian, though being a Pole somewhat undermines this advantage. After writing a letter to Slipyi in which he declared that the Ukrainians, too, had the right to religious liberty, he prepared for the future by ordaining personally on 12 November in the Sistine Chapel the new Ukrainian Metropolitan of Philadelphia. Miroslav Lubachivsky was known to be opposed to the idea of creating a new patriarchate.

Two Slavs not quite eye-to-eye: a ritual embrace for Ukrainian Cardinal Josef Slipyi.

So his appointment displeased Slipyi and his followers. But at Lubachivsky's ordination, John Paul went out of his way to praise Slipyi's heroism. 'The whole modern world', he said, 'knows of the outstanding witness which, by your arduous life and your many years of imprisonment, you have given to Jesus Christ and to the Church born of his cross and resurrection.' This was gratifying to Slipyi and the Ukrainians, for it was an endorsement of one of their favourite themes: that the Passion of Christ was today being relived in the Ukraine. Slav speaks to Slav. But that was not all John Paul said. He added: 'With all my heart I wish to ensure the internal unity of your Church and its unity with the See of Peter.'

With an Eastern ikon looking ill at ease in the Renaissance splendour of the Sistine Chapel, Pope John Paul presides over a Mass with the Ukrainian bishops, while the 88-year-old Cardinal Slipyi (centre left) apparently holds the stage.

This desire was fulfilled by the calling of the Synod four months later. Unlike the Dutch Synod, it was brief—only four days. There were no leaks and it had only one objective: to present to the Pope a list of names for the nomination of an auxiliary or assistant bishop to Cardinal Slipyi *with right of succession*. The last phrase was crucial. It meant that the Ukrainians were choosing their next Major Archbishop. They were free, but only up to a point, for they would have to choose someone acceptable to the Pope. At the conclusion of the Synod it was announced, to the surprise of no one, that Metropolitan Lubachivsky had been appointed. That meant that, though controversy would rumble on in the Ukrainian émigré press, the question of the patriarchate was now resolved—negatively.

So some sort of peace was restored to the badly-buffeted Ukrainian Church. But a price may have to be paid for it that was not realised at the time. The Ukrainian Catholic Church is a

West and East – the difference of apparel is more than a matter of 'tradition': the word itself is pronounced differently . . .

'Uniate Church' (though it detests the term), that is, a Church with its own rites and traditions which is nevertheless in full communion with the Bishop of Rome. Many ecumenists have thought that the Uniate model is the way ahead for other Churches not yet in communion with Rome. But this would only be possible if the Uniate Churches were seen to have real autonomy. The lesson of the Ukrainian Synod was that their area of independence is extremely limited.

10 *African Safari*

Pope John Paul being greeted by President Mobutu on arrival in Zaire. The six-foot-two balding man in dark glasses to the Pope's right is his bodyguard, the American Monsignor Paul Marcinkus, who is also his financial consultant . . .

John Paul II was not the first pope to visit Africa. In 1969 Paul VI went to Uganda, but he stayed only three days, did not go far from the capital, Kampala, and made only a few (but some important) speeches. In contrast John Paul was in Africa for ten days, delivered just over seventy sermons and addresses, and visited six countries: Zaire, the People's Republic of the Congo, Kenya, Upper Volta, Ghana and the Ivory Coast. It was his most ambitious, exhausting and exhilarating journey so far.

The settings changed kaleidoscopically: stifling heat in the equatorial forests of Zaire and Congo, the temperate rolling hill country of Kenya, a tropical thunderstorm in Ghana, desert dryness around Ouagadougou, capital of Upper Volta, where John Paul made a forceful appeal for the victims of famine and drought.

Other differences came from the lingering colonial past. Though impoverished, the People's Republic of the Congo has a touch of French *panache* and Abidjan, capital of the Ivory Coast, resembles a Mediterranean city—except that it has blue lagoons

Another mode of welcome: dancing girls at Nairobi airport.

as well. At Nairobi airport there were flower beds, awnings for the dignitaries, large ladies in even larger hats, a superb brass band and Brigade of Guards drill, while in Ghana there were burly policemen in British-style uniforms and Anglican choir-girls in Canterbury caps and blue academic gowns.

What did not change was the generous African welcome, the sheer spontaneous and exuberant delight of peoples who, for

65

'I am the Lord of the Dance', maybe?

Not a ticker-tape ride in downtown Houston, Texas, despite the hat. Actually Kisangani, Zaire.

the most part, are not visited by anyone of international importance. So they danced and danced and played their exciting music.

The visit had a serious purpose as well. John Paul spent more time—five days—in Zaire than anywhere else. Strategically it was the most important country he visited since it has the greatest number of bishops (56) and the largest population, 22 million, half of which is Roman Catholic. It was in Kinshasa, capital of Zaire, that John Paul delivered his main message to the Church in Africa; and as usual, he reserved his most important remarks for the address to the bishops. He stressed the limits of 'Africanisation'. The term is unclear and ambiguous, he pointed out, 'for it covers vast areas, many of which have not been properly explored.' They would have to learn to be patient and to bide their time. Poland, he said, had taken ten centuries to assimilate Christian faith. It seemed an incongruous comparison in the equatorial heat, but it was meant to introduce a personal touch.

The central question in the debate about Africanisation concerns the relationship between Christianity and the local African cultures. The early missionaries simply rejected the local culture or denounced it as superstitious and corrupt. Political independence led many African Christians to take another look at their own traditions and seek ways of adapting them to

Still not quite the African style of headgear, but an appreciative crowd being introduced by Cardinal Joseph Malula of Kinshasa, Zaire.

Christianity. In this way they could be both loyal citizens and the faith would be truly 'incarnated' in Africa.

John Paul, however, saw dangers in too much adaptation too hastily adopted. The liturgy, he said, should maintain 'a substantial unity with the Roman rite', and any innovations should be approved and 'dignified'. As for theology, it could not be reduced to a synthesis between the Gospel message and the local culture which would simply omit and ignore the traditional (and largely European) ways in which faith had been expressed. Again, though lay catechists have a vital role, the ordained priest, male and celibate, remained the principal agent of evangelisation. (Cardinal Joseph Malula's desire to ordain those married men who are in fact the real builders of the local community was not even mentioned: it will make no headway in this pontificate.) The same principles were applied to marriage customs. In an address to young couples in Kinshasa, John Paul went to his favourite first chapters of Genesis to show that monogamous marriage as a life-long and equal partnership was a God-given idea (and not, therefore, as some Africans have been suggesting, a 'European invention' which did not apply to them). Africans were perfectly capable of this high ideal, and standards must not be lowered. John Paul constantly stressed that being a Christian meant being *converted*: it could not mean carrying on as before, but under a different label.

All in all, it was a stern lecture that John Paul read out. It was as though he had gone to Africa to take a firm grip on a situation that was in danger of getting out of hand. Hardly anyone managed to identify the white-haired cardinal who was seen everywhere with the Pope. It was in fact the Brazilian Angelo Rossi who is the Prefect of the Congregation for the Evangelisation of Peoples (its older, more convenient name, Propaganda, was abandoned for obvious reasons). It is responsible for all young Churches, including those of Africa. Cardinal Rossi is a known opponent of 'Africanisation', especially as it was being worked out in Zaire.

John Paul shares this judgement. So he was unable to repeat what Paul VI had said in Kampala: 'You can and must have an African Christianity.' On the other hand, he did recognize that African cultural elements, suitably 'refined and purified', could be introduced into Christianity. The missionary has to start from what is there. John Paul spoke of the 'values of African society' as the necessary basis for all evangelisation. His 'image' of Africa was stated in classical form in his speech to the President of Ghana on 8 May:

One of the original aspects of this continent is its diversity, but a diversity that is bound together by the undeniable unity of its culture: a vision of the world where the sacred is central; a deep awareness of the link between Creator and nature; a great respect for all life; a sense of family and of community that blossoms into an open and joyous hospitality; reverence for dialogue as a means of settling differences; spontaneity and the joy of living expressed in poetic language, song and dance.

This is a possible though somewhat selective and optimistic presentation of 'African values'. John Paul insisted that 'the African soul', a term no longer used by anthropologists and disliked by many Africans, was 'naturally religious' if not

Papal throne, African style.

68

'naturally Christian': an important claim in a continent where Islam and Marxism are also at work.

However, one should not exaggerate the solemnity of the visit. It was up river in Kisangani (formerly Stanleyville) that the

An enthusiastic crowd with some latter-day Zacchaeuses.

whole mood began to change. Cheerfulness broke in. The heavy lectures prepared in advance were passing over the heads of many of his listeners, who did not all have a good command of French. In Kisangani, John Paul evidently decided that he might as well enjoy himself. As he stepped off the plane he beat time to the welcoming music, and eventually essayed a sideways shuffle with the teenage girls dressed in papal white and gold. It was just enough to be able to say 'the Pope danced'. The disaster in Kinshasa, where nine people had been crushed or trampled to death while waiting for the Pope, now seemed far away.

The many open-air Masses were joyous celebrations. John Paul was able to judge for himself whether the African liturgy has retained 'a substantial unity with the Roman rite'. It has, but at the same time it is adding elements of its own. In Kinshasa, for example, before the Chinese-built People's Palace, twenty

The celebration in front of the People's Palace in Kinshasa.

Zairian priests in golden chasubles danced round the altar during the *Gloria*, swaying rhythmically from side to side, their hands outstretched in self-offering. The invitation, 'let us pray', was almost everywhere the signal for the tom-toms to beat out, solemnly and reverently, and the offertory procession provided a chance for yet more song and dance. In Abidjan the women danced up the altar steps with baskets of local produce nimbly balanced on their heads. The travelling papal master of ceremonies, Mgr Virgilio Noè, mopped his brow and wondered what to do with so much fruit.

Hats again – and the Pope deciding that mitres are preferable after all.

It was difficult to gauge John Paul's response. For the most part he smiled benevolently and seemed to be concentrating hard on his prayers. At Uhuru Park in Nairobi he accepted a spear and donned a headdress, traditional symbols of authority. But that was after the Mass was over. In his farewell speech at Abidjan (it had been written in advance) he said how impressed he had been by meeting 'living communities, so full of enthusiasm and imagination'. 'Imagination', he added, 'is a virtue we don't pay enough attention to.' It was the first papal commendation of imagination since the Renaissance.

The most spectacular encounter was with the King of the Ashanti in the sports stadium at Kumasi, Ghana. Red and gold parasols protected the King and some two hundred gnarled noblemen. A servant waved a wicker-work fan to keep the King cool, another whisked away flies with a cow's tail, while a third

The King of the Ashanti and entourage.

mopped up the sweat that trickled down the royal back. Guards with muskets that must have served in the Ashanti Wars brought up the rear. It was almost a disappointment to discover that the King is a London-trained lawyer and that he has been an Anglican from the age of five.

But John Paul had other meetings that were less spectacular and yet more politically significant. His message to Africa as a whole was given in a speech to the diplomatic corps in Nairobi. He said that Africa could and should be allowed to solve its own problems, without interference from the outside. His vision is of a 'neutralised' Africa, rid of the imported conflicts of the super-powers. The Pope's remarks were directed even-handedly against the 'consumerism' of the West and the materialism of communism. John Paul was in Africa in the very week in which President Tito of Yugoslavia died and was buried. So one could say that the torch of non-alignment, laid down by Tito, was picked up by the Pope in Africa.

Of more immediate concern during the visit was the risk that local leaders would exploit it to strengthen their own positions.

President Mobutu and his bride: 'pastoral first-fruits'.

This was particularly true in Zaire and Ivory Coast where Presidents Mobutu and Houphouët-Boigny took good care to be seen with John Paul as often as possible. By a remarkable coincidence, both of them got married shortly before the Pope's arrival—Mobutu the day before, Houphouët-Boigny a week before. This anxiety to 'put things right with the Church' seemed significant. In the plane on the way home I asked John Paul about this last-minute rush into matrimony. He laughed. Then he said: 'I don't think they got married out of courtesy towards me. Let us say that these marriages were the first fruits of my pastoral visit to Africa.' There the matter was left.

Both the newly-weds run one-party states and have not always been gentle in dealing with potential opposition. John Paul made no critical comments on one-party regimes, and confined himself to saying (in the allegedly Marxist People's Republic of the Congo) that the Church was 'not tied to any particular form of political or social organisation'. But there might still be reasons for preferring one form to another. The American Ambassador in Ouagadougou regretted that John Paul had not mentioned the fact that Upper Volta had a democratically elected President, an official opposition, and no political prisoners.

On the other hand, John Paul got a rousing cheer every time he used the word 'corruption'. The trouble with the one-party state is that jobs and contracts go to the members of the old-boy network. The other problem is that there is no way to remove the revered father of the nation except by a *coup d'état*. There were persistent though unfounded rumours that the military were going to strike in Abidjan while the President was busy acting as John Paul's guide to the Ivory Coast.

Abidjan was the last stop in Africa. Before leaving, John Paul summed up the lessons of his journey. 'For ten days', he said, 'I have been the astonished and thunder-struck (*bouleversé*) witness of the vitality of the young Churches of Africa. I invite the whole Church, especially the ancient Churches of Christendom, to look upon their sister Churches with esteem and confidence.' No longer 'daughter Churches', dependent on the West for missionaries and money, the Churches of Africa have reached a stage of maturity that was recognised by the

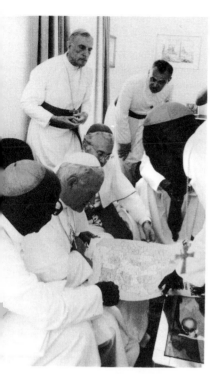

Pastoral strategy on the Ivory Coast.

Religious enthusiasm well under way: a vast banner of the Sacred Heart overshadowing another of the Pope.

papal visit. The logical next step would be to release them from the tutelage of the Congregation for the Evangelisation of Peoples. But that is unlikely to happen. Meanwhile, the effect of the visit was to put Africa on the Christian map and its problems on the agenda of the universal Church.

11   *How far to Canterbury?*

The Pope and Archbishop Robert Runcie of Canterbury: next time they meet will be on English soil.

At seven o'clock on the morning of 9 May, Pope John Paul II met Dr Robert Runcie, the recently-enthroned Archbishop of Canterbury, in Accra, capital of Ghana. That may seem an uncivilised hour for an ecumenical chat, but in the African heat it is the last moment when one is likely to have a clear head. The joint statement suggested that Accra was a good place to meet because the view from Africa sets the conflicts inherited from Europe in due perspective.

Pope and Archbishop declared: 'The time is too short and the need too pressing to waste Christian energies pursuing old rivalries, and that the talents and resources of all the Christian Churches must be shared if Christ is to be seen and heard effectively'. Together they endorsed the commitment of their predecessors to ecumenism: 'Common action depends on progress in the "serious dialogue", now nearly fourteen years established, by which Roman Catholics and Anglicans have been seeking the way to that unity of faith and communion which Christ wills for his Church'. The meeting in Accra had established a basis of personal friendship and trust upon which Pope and Archbishop 'intend to build in a fuller meeting in the future.'

The papal visit to England in 1982 will doubtless provide the time and place for such a meeting. So apparently everything in the Anglican/Catholic garden of dialogue is flourishing. It is not churlish to point out that there are also a few thorns. Observers are already asking whether the 1982 tour will produce a practical step forward for Church unity or merely sincere but symbolic expressions of good will.

John Paul's constant stress on a clear statement of Catholic identity means that his version of ecumenism is rather different from that of Paul VI. He is no less committed to it, but he has a different background and a different style. He never tires of saying that the way ahead involves above all 'spiritual renewal' rather than theological compromise, and that though unity is willed by the Holy Spirit, we do not yet know what form it will take or when it will be realised. Moreover, as we have already seen, dialogue with the Orthodox counts for more with him than dialogue with the Churches which emerged from the Reformation. Partly this is a question of relative unfamiliarity.

On the way to Africa I asked John Paul whether he would use the term 'Sister Church' in speaking of the Anglican Communion. It had been used several times by Paul VI and

75

A cloistered view of Rome . . .

could be construed as a declaration of some sort of equality. 'I don't know', he began, 'I think, I think . . . I must say till this time I did not much think about this denomination.' Those were the exact words, in English. There was an evident ambiguity. Was John Paul confessing his ignorance about Anglicans or saying that he has not given much thought to the designation 'Sister Church'? He went on: 'But we are all brothers and sisters in the Lord. In the Council documents "Sister Church" is only an analogy.' Again, there was a puzzle: did this mean that no theological conclusions can be drawn from the use of the term?

Official statements are not much clearer than these *obiter dicta*. The Anglican/Roman Catholic Theological Commission has all but completed its work. Its three joint reports (on the Eucharist, Ministry and Authority) together with the volume called *Elucidations* which answered objections to them, will shortly be presented to the respective 'authorities' for further action. In a speech to the Secretariat for Christian Unity John Paul noted that the work would be completed in 1981 and commented: 'The Catholic Church will then be able to pronounce officially and draw the consequences for the next stage.'

The problem is to know what 'the Catholic Church' means in that last sentence. Just who, in this case, are its 'authorities'? The Anglican answer is straightforward. The Agreed Statements will be debated and reported upon by the Synods of

the twenty-seven Churches that make up the world-wide
Anglican Communion. No one has so far stated who the
corresponding Catholic 'authorities' are. The idea was floated
that perhaps a special Synod should be called, made up of
bishops who have experience of Anglicans and ecumenical work
generally. But after the experience of the Dutch and Ukrainian
special Synods, enthusiasm for this idea waned.

A clue to John Paul's attitude to ecumenism came in a letter he
wrote to the Presbyterian Church of Ireland. During his visit to
Dublin he had been presented with a document written by the
Presbyterians who lamented the lack of progress made on their
ecumenical front. There was no time to discuss it there and
then. But five months later the Presbyterians were gratified to
receive a written reply. John Paul defined dialogue as 'a process
of making oneself understood and seeking to understand'. No
trouble about that. But he went on:

*Inevitably such dialogue must first involve a small group of qualified
representatives of either Church, but once they arrive at consensus, it
remains difficult to translate words into actions until the results of the
dialogue have been communicated to the members of the Churches at
every level, often by a process which is itself a form of dialogue.*

This was said in the context of the Catholic/Presbyterian
dialogue in Ireland, but it reflects a broader assessment of the

ecumenical scene. In John Paul's mind there are three conditions for a successful dialogue defined as the restoration of full communion. It should not be left in the hands of experts or theologians. It involves the preparation of the ordinary Christians on both sides. And this pedagogical process cannot be rushed.

The emphasis on Catholic identity and warnings against surrendering to experts and undue haste combine to slow down the pace of the ecumenical movement. But they do not halt it altogether. It could even be argued that they inject a note of pastoral realism and common sense into dialogues that have sometimes been the work of enthusiastic professionals of ecumenism. On the other hand this does not mean pouring cold water on their efforts, without which complete immobility would reign. John Paul has many times expressed his gratitude for the progress already made.

For example, at the General Audience of 25 June he commented on the 450th anniversary of the Confession of Augsburg that was being celebrated at that time. In its day it had been an attempt at *rapprochement*. But it failed, and thereafter the break between Lutherans and Catholics seemed irreparable for centuries. The situation has now changed. John Paul said: 'Our gratitude is all the greater because we can see now with more clarity than was possible at the time that even though the building of the bridge failed, the tempest of time has spared some of its most important pillars.'

It may be that the strong assertion of Catholic identity is less of a drawback to the ecumenical movement than it might seem at first sight. Some Lutherans at Augsburg were impelled to ask themselves: 'Why are we Lutherans, given that we can no longer be Lutherans for the reasons advanced by Luther?' Others went further still: 'Why are we not Roman Catholics, given that the Roman Catholic Church has largely reformed itself on the matters which aroused the wrath of Luther?'

Every Church, in short, has to define itself, to state its identity, before it can engage in dialogue. By his ecumenical attitudes, by his intransigeance even, John Paul II has forced such questions out into the open.

12 *Weekend in Paris*

A Pope in Paris for the first time since Napoleon's era.

Less than three weeks after his return from Africa, John Paul was off again, this time for a long weekend in Paris. He looked at his programme a fortnight before and exclaimed, in substance: 'But there is no meeting with intellectuals. Everywhere I go I meet intellectuals. Arrange a meeting with intellectuals.' There are, of course, plenty of intellectuals available in Paris. A selection of them went along for breakfast with the Pope at the Nunciature, 10 Avenue Wilson, on Saturday 31 May. According to André Frossard, author of *God exists—I've met Him,* who was present, John Paul simply asked questions. He opened with: 'What do you think of the way the world is going?' Not surprisingly, an hour later they had not managed to complete their *tour de table*. The pontifical breakfast was over. Uninvited intellectuals complained afterwards that the Pope's guests were 'somewhat of the right'.

Musical chairs – no doubt in the interests of good communication.

Later that same morning 3,000 'personalities' were invited to a Garden Party at the Elysée Palace, home and office of President Valéry Giscard d'Estaing. But the scudding rain drove everyone indoors and the crush was frightful to behold. Some of the guests leaped out of the windows to escape asphyxiation. Ladies lost their shoes in the rhododendron bushes. Those who persisted strained to catch the exchanges between Georges Marchais, First Secretary of the French Communist Party, and John Paul. They were rewarded with Marchais saying, 'May I present my wife, Holy Father?' Then they reminisced a little about a mutual Polish friend, Edward Gierek, then still in power, since 'invalided out'. Before the war he had worked in the coal mines of Northern France. Keen-eyed observers noted that the Pope seized both hands of Marchais. But it was all rather insignificant and disappointing.

So the pontifical visit to France went on, poised between windiness and platitude. The primary reason for John Paul's journey was to address UNESCO which has its headquarters in Paris. But he could not decently go there without also visiting the French Church, however cursorily. At lunch in the Vatican

The Pope at UNESCO, being greeted by its director-general, Amadou Mahtar M'Bow of Senegal.

when the trip was being planned, he asked the Nuncio in Paris, Archbishop Angelo Felici: 'Do people really want to see me in France?' The Nuncio reassured him. All would be well.

Certainly the satirists enjoyed the visit. The newspapers were full of ironical cartoons. In one of them the Pope was seen presenting Marianne, symbol of France. 'Let me introduce my eldest daughter,' he was saying. On his other side was a little black girl. *Libération*, the socialist daily, had a spoof issue. Page one was entirely dominated by a portrait of John Paul. In the corner one read: 'This paper has been impregnated with the odour of sanctity: sniff it for yourself.' I saw several people in the Métro taking a surreptitious sniff. *Le Monde*, the most intellectual of French newspapers, balanced its accounts of the visit with articles by atheists and free-thinkers who enquired whether John Paul really believed what he said. To some extent these were predictable attacks from predictable sources. But the mood of sophisticated scepticism was not confined to anti-clericals: it was found in Church circles too, especially among the militant Catholic Actionists and the politically committed who did not like John Paul's conservatism.

The French bishops had bad luck. It was not they who had suggested that the Mass at Le Bourget airport on the Sunday morning would be a rally, a kind of plebiscite which would show that despite the ravages of secularisation, Christianity was still firmly rooted in the nation. That was what the newspapers had said. A million and a half had been confidently expected before the visit. The estimate was down to a million on the day John Paul arrived. In the end about 350,000 people turned up, many of them elderly folk from the provinces.

Umbrellas the order of the day at Le Bourget.

But neither the newspapers nor the Bishops had counted on the weather. On this first day of June, the temperature during the night fell to below freezing. During the Mass, the wind blew and the rain poured down intermittently. There is nothing quite so desolate as an abandoned airport in the rain. The bedraggled banners and the red shirts of the European scouts, who did the marshalling, provided the only colour. At one point all one could see of the altar was a white umbrella surrounded by a cluster of black umbrellas.

Nevertheless, John Paul read out his forty-five minute sermon. In it he denounced, though not of course by name, the existentialism of Jean-Paul Sartre: 'The problem of the absence of Christ does not exist. The problem of his relegation to the margins of human history does not exist. The silence of God with regard to the restlessness and fate of man does not exist.' The homily ended with a question: 'France, eldest daughter of the Church, are you faithful to your baptismal promises?' The title 'eldest daughter of the Church' makes most French Catholics smile or wince. It was based on the fact that Clovis, in the fifth century, was the first of the barbarian kings to be converted to Christianity. It was revived in the middle of the nineteenth century when papal zouaves were being recruited to fight against the Italian reunification movement. It has become the slogan of the right wing in France. Cardinal François Marty, on the verge of retirement as Archbishop of Paris, never uses it.

But John Paul insisted on using the expression and showed that his image of France belongs to the past. Secularisation, he told the French bishops later that same day, is not an irreversible process. With a little more resolution and courage they could roll it back. Like de Gaulle, John Paul has 'a certain idea of France'. It goes hand-in-hand with his map of Italy, sketched out earlier. It is the France of saints like the Curé d'Ars and Theresa of Lisieux (whither he also went). It is the France of pilgrimages and great abbeys and monastic foundations. It is the France of heroic missionary endeavour and countless mother foundresses. It is the France of nostalgic memory rather than present experience.

Cardinal Roger Etchegaray, Archbishop of Marseilles, said later, 'The Pope's visit enabled us to see ourselves more clearly.' But even he must have been aware of the gulf between his own speech of welcome to John Paul and the Pope's reply.

Love is – sheltering your fellow-concelebrant at Mass.

Etchegaray offered a positive interpretation of secularisation. He conceded that increasing numbers of French people now go through life in complete ignorance of religion. But this means that the believer, 'no longer able to rely on the institutional or social crutches of the past, has to rely on God alone.' As the analysis differed, so too did the remedies proposed.

Notre Dame de Paris, Papal style.

John Paul's main practical advice to the French bishops was that they should exercise keener vigilance over theological publications, especially those that filter down to the masses. 'They can', he declared, 'shake or dissolve faith by their partiality or their methods.' No doubt. But that is not the first priority of the French Bishops. They know the statistics. Though 80 per cent of French people are baptized, only 15 per cent practise their religion (measured by the test of weekly Mass attendance). They know that priests are getting older and that vocations are simply not there. They know that although there are still 365 congregations of women religious in France, between them they have only 200 novices.

The gap between French experience and John Paul's perception of it was vividly illustrated in the Mass celebrated at Saint Denis, burial place of French kings and now a working-class suburb with a numerous immigrant population. The specially prepared liturgy was a hymn to working-class solidarity and the struggle for justice. The prayer of the faithful evoked the plight of the Métro cleaners who had been on strike for twenty-one days. The Communist mayor and the immigrants waited patiently in the square outside the basilica. A large banner proclaimed the slogan of Cardinal Cardijn, founder of the Young Christian Workers: 'A young worker is worth all the gold in the world.'

The Pope at prayer in the basilica of Lisieux.

The Mass was inside the basilica but the homily was, curiously, outside. John Paul began by denouncing abortion (it was the feast of the Annunciation, and the text about Elizabeth's child leaping in the womb proved irresistible). The mayor cheered up a little when John Paul moved on to the dignity of work. As an old worker himself, he knew that work had value because it was done 'for others', for the family. It was a sketch of his next encyclical, probably for 1981, the ninetieth anniversary of *Rerum*

Novarum, Leo XIII's 'social encyclical'. Family and work were closely linked. 'The rights of the family', he said, 'should be written into the legislation which governs work.' Working women posed a problem.

But the struggle for justice should not be identified with the class-war. The mayor took this on the chin. 'The world of work must be a world of love and not hatred,' said John Paul, even though he went on to quote the *Magnificat* about 'casting down the powerful from their thrones' and 'sending the rich away empty-handed'.

The liturgy and the homily seemed to be pointing in different directions. Everyone noticed that the three points of the homily—work, family and nation—echoed the motto of the wartime Pétain regime, deliberately chosen in opposition to the 1789 revolutionary slogan, 'Liberty, Equality and Fraternity'. It is true that the next day, at Le Bourget, John Paul tried to 'recuperate' liberty, equality and fraternity for Christianity. These were, he explained, fundamentally Christian ideas, even if the revolutionaries specifically rejected Christianity. But by then the damage had been done. John Paul had used the Pétainist, right-wing slogan.

The one indubitable success of the visit was the meeting with young people at Parc des Princes, a sports stadium, on Sunday 1 June. 50 thousand were crammed inside, while another 35 thousand listened from beyond the fence. They had seen on television the meetings with young people at Galway and Madison Square Garden, and were determined to show that French *jeunes* could make just as much noise. Cardinal Marty introduced John Paul as 'God's sportsman', and he said himself that he wanted a dialogue. So young people came to the microphone and asked questions or made statements.

What can young people do to prevent a third World War? Why is there evil in the world? Why doesn't the Church recognize the immense resource it has in the enthusiasm of youth? How can you be so certain about the faith? Now and then there was a hint of the charismatic. 'God is marvellous, genial, fantastic,' said one young girl, 'whenever I think of him I want to dance and sing.' Then up stepped a young man who said: 'I am an atheist.'

(Boos and whistles from an intolerant section of the crowd.) 'I don't understand faith. I can think of no one better than you to explain it to me. Who is this God whom you adore?'

John Paul read out his speech. It had been prepared in advance, though the first draft had been discarded. He didn't answer all the questions. But it didn't matter in the slightest. The point was to celebrate youth as the hope of the future. It was vague and it set the pulses racing. We never discovered whether the young atheist was converted.

Montmartre, window on the Parisian world.

But the vignette which summed up the weekend in Paris was the unscheduled visit later that same night to the Basilica of the Sacred Heart in Montmartre. John Paul got there well after midnight. The night clubs and—for all I know—the brothels poured out their clientèle to see this unaccustomed and extraordinary sight: the Pope in Montmartre. From the top of the hill, in total darkness, John Paul blessed the unsleeping city and the largely unheeding nation. Meanwhile President Giscard d'Estaing claimed that in private conversation John Paul had approved his initiative in going to meet Leonid Brezhnev in Warsaw to keep alive the flickering flame of *détente*. Life went on. John Paul won over many by his charm and evident sincerity. But there will be further trouble from the 'eldest daughter of the Church'.

13 *Church and Politics in Brazil*

Pause for thought on arrival in Brazil: the Pope with the Brazilian president, João Figueiredo.

Anyone who imagined that John Paul's journey to Africa had attained the limits of human endurance only needed to go with him to Brazil to be disabused: there were yet new heights to be scaled. It was a twelve-day visit early in July with every kind of climate from the allegedly temperate (but in fact bitterly cold) to the undeniably tropical. Brazil is in effect a sub-continent in which everything is huge: the distances, the cities, the rivers, the forests and the problems.

It is a country that has made a great economic 'leap forwards' in the last fifteen years but is now in the grip of inflation and recession. Side by side are extremes of wealth and extremes of poverty. Its capital, Brasilia, is a science-fiction attempt to build a twenty-first century city, while in the Amazonian forests anthropologists study some of the world's most ancient cultures, now rapidly disappearing.

Bring on the dancing girls.

It is by far the largest country in South America, and of its 120 million population just over 90 per cent are baptized Roman Catholics. 330 bishops make up the world's biggest Episcopal Conference and, many would say, the most effective. A fair case can be made for saying that it was the first and remains the most genuinely multi-racial society in existence. Only a year before John Paul had quoted with approval the remark: 'Humanly speaking, the future of the Church is being played out in Latin America.' Which explains why he wanted to visit it.

He had already taken a sighting-shot at Central and Latin American problems by going to Mexico in February 1979. But that visit remained ambivalent in that both the advocates and the opponents of liberation theology could plausibly claim to have the Pope on their side. Meanwhile, events had not stood still. Christians had played an important part in the revolution in Nicaragua which overthrew the dictator, General Somoza: it was the first instance of liberation theology in action, providing an alternative left-wing model to the Chile of Allende and the

Cuba of Castro—there were five priests in its first cabinet. (Later, the Bishops ordered them to withdraw 'as soon as possible', but that moment has not yet arrived.) The murder of Archbishop Oskar Romero in El Salvador had dramatised the truth that those who 'opt for the poorest' must expect to get killed. John Paul disappointed many by speaking of this murder as 'sacrilege' rather than as 'martyrdom'.

All these problems were reflected in Brazil. But in addition Brazil had its own set of special difficulties which complicated the papal visit and, at one time, nearly led to its postponement. The Church was becoming increasingly the only rallying-point for opposition to the military government of President João Figueiredo. In the three months before John Paul arrived, the Brazilian bishops had annoyed the government by supporting the metal workers' strike in São Paolo, by publishing a long and controversial document on the urgency of land reform, and by denouncing the unjust expropriation of the few remaining Indians. The government had angrily responded by dismissing the protesting bishops as 'subversive clerics' and claiming that they were 'unrepresentative of the Church as a whole'. Misled by the nuncio in Brasilia, the government may have counted on pontifical coolness towards the 'political' bishops, if not their condemnation.

Bring on the bishops.

In fact John Paul brought the prestige of his office and the charisma of his personality to the support of the bishops. In the immense football stadium of São Paolo, he publicly embraced Cardinal Evaristo Arns, the government's *bête noire*, defended the right of workers to band together in trades unions, and said, pointedly: 'I speak in the name of Christ, in the name of the Church, in the name of the whole Church.' So much for the argument that the offending clerics were 'unrepresentative'.

In Recife there was an affectionate embrace for Archbishop Helder Camara, the man who has been so frequently described in the Brazilian papers as a 'communist'; and there John Paul pledged his support for the land-reform project of the Brazilian bishops.

Problems of communication, it would appear, with an Indian chief at Manaus, on the Amazon. The chief was presenting the Pope with a wooden cross and a spear.

Finally the Pope went up the Amazon to Manaus to ensure that the case of the Indians would not go by default ('One should not speak of "the discovery of Brazil",' they told him, 'for we existed as a people before the Europeans arrived.') It was a point-by-point vindication of the social policies of the Brazilian bishops. No wonder they were overjoyed. Helder Camara was asked: 'What will you do now?' He was able to answer: 'We will carry on as before.' Another bishop said: 'If any one of us had spoken out as strongly as the Pope did, he would be in jail by now.' Papal immunity and popular support enabled John Paul to say what he liked. 'John, John, John of God,' they cried incautiously, 'you are our king.'

So the visit was in an obvious sense a challenge to the government. John Paul repeatedly spoke of Brazil as 'a radically Catholic nation' which as such has 'a special vocation in the contemporary world and in the whole concert of nations'. The special vocation is to devise a new and alternative model of

Visiting a Brazilian *favela* or shanty town.

society which would be neither capitalist nor communist. It would be based rather on 'Catholic social doctrine'. So the stakes of the visit were high. John Paul wanted to give history a push—away from the class-war and towards justice and participation. Only in an ostensibly Catholic country could such an ambition be taken seriously.

However, John Paul also insisted that the Church is not concerned with party politics or with precise political nostrums. But it has the right and the duty to lay down the principles which flow immediately from its doctrine of 'man' and his unique dignity. The government could be forgiven for finding this distinction paradoxical and hard to grasp. For as soon as Catholic social principles are 'cashed', they issue in reforms—and an imprecise reform is no reform at all.

Porto Alegre, Brazil: politics as etched on the faces of these mothers and wives of Argentinians who have 'disappeared' for political reasons.

The same distinction (between asserting principles and applying them in practice) was the reason why John Paul could insist on the exclusion of clerics from the political rough and tumble. In Rio de Janeiro on 2 July he ordained seventy-four priests (which may sound a lot but is less than one per million of the Catholic population) and told them that 'the role of the priest is not that of doctor, social worker, politician or trade-unionist', even though, in the past, they may have performed some of these roles admirably. But that was only because competent laymen were not available. In future priests must confine themselves to announcing principles, leaving practical politics to the laity.

At this point the government could begin to breathe again. For one of its constant themes was precisely that 'priests should stay out of politics', and here was the Pope endorsing their judgement. Moreover, in his speech to the Brazilian bishops, John Paul stressed the 'primacy of the spiritual' (a phrase that is anathema to liberation theologians). Using a familiar rhetorical device, he said that he had received many letters from Brazil, touching in their simplicity, which revealed 'a hunger for God, an openness to the sacred, a thirst for the truth of the Gospel and for the supernatural life'. He did not report that his correspondents made any political demands. Presumably they did not. The point of mentioning them, therefore, was to assert once again 'the primacy of the spiritual' with the implication that this had been somewhat neglected.

There was another reason why the government could take heart. In his speech to President Figueiredo John Paul called for 'speedy reforms' and darkly hinted that this was the only way to prevent them being sought 'under the influence of ideological systems that do not hesitate to have recourse to violence and the suppression of the liberty and rights that are fundamental to the dignity of man.' In other words: reform now—or reap the Marxist whirlwind soon.

That may sound like common sense. But it provided the government with an alibi for inaction. It made the fear of subversion a legitimate motive—and that is the basis of the 'national security state', the theory that anything goes where the interests of the state are concerned. Suppose that the Brazilian government made concessions on trade-union activity, as John Paul recommended. Does that mean that they can go on strike?—not that the Pope mentioned strikes. And if the workers responded to the first concessions by asking for more, then the government could choose to regard this as the first ripple that would lead to the avalanche of revolution. The longed-for 'reforms' would be indefinitely delayed because the people are not 'ready' for them.

This was, then, the first issue on which a gap opened up between John Paul and the Brazilian bishops. They believe that injustice must be denounced because it is intolerable. Period. And their 'option for the poorest' means more than paternalistically 'defending their rights' or making speeches about their unhappy fate. It means being with them in the *favelas* or shanty-towns and making them aware, simultaneously, of what they can do for themselves and why the Gospel is relevant. It means, in some sense, 'people-power'. This has been the basis of the theology of liberation. But where governments are urged to 'reforms', the unspoken assumption is that it is only they who act in history, and that the 'people' are merely the objects of their wise and beneficent action.

A boy from Rio de Janeiro's Vidigal slum kisses the gold ring which Pope John Paul II donated to the local parish when he visited it.

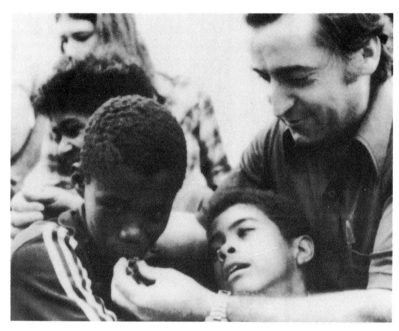

A comparable difference soon became apparent in the sphere of Church life. The Brazilian bishops had wanted to ordain married men, chosen among the natural leaders of the 'basic communities'. They were sharply told that they could not. 'Do not delude yourselves', John Paul said, 'that a priesthood less rigorous in its demands of sacrifice and renunciation—as for example in the demands of priestly celibacy—would increase the number of those who want to commit themselves to the following of Christ.' But that was not quite what the bishops had been arguing for. They did not dream that they were 'lowering standards', and in any case the sacrifice and renunciation involved in living in a *favela* are considerable. Their intention had been to find pastorally acceptable ways of satisfying the hunger for the sacraments, and especially for the Eucharist.

The Brazilian bishops were called to order on another point. They had defended Fr Leonardo Boff against the Congregation for the Doctrine of Faith. John Paul reminded them that communion with the Pope is expressed by accepting his words not only when he speaks personally, but when they come through the organs that collaborate with him in the pastoral government of the Church and which speak in his name, with his approval or with his mandate. He could hardly have said more clearly that the Roman Curia must be obeyed.

An ecumenical gathering: dissident Catholic theologians are not addressed quite so fraternally.

Nor did John Paul accept the notion that the danger of theological error could be brushed aside. 'We would all be happy', he told the bishops, 'if the errors and deviations in the areas of Christ, Church and man were remote possibilities, not in evidence at the moment. But you all know that such is not the case.' No list of 'errors and deviations' was provided. But certainly the Brazilian bishops' emphasis on 'basic communities', so often regarded by them as the hope and the future of the Church, was not echoed by John Paul. He spoke about them rarely and then only with apprehension, stressing the dangers and contrasting them with the parish which he held to be the ordinary *locus* of apostolic activity.

But it little mattered what he said about 'basic communities'. He contributed to this debate by the mere fact of going to Brazil and assembling such vast and enthusiastic crowds everywhere. In so doing, he reminded the Brazilian bishops that there exists a popular or mass religion that they could build upon. Of course, as he conceded, it may be to some extent superstitious and it certainly requires constantly renewed catechesis, but it is there as a largely untapped social force and could transform Brazil by making it truly a 'Catholic nation'.

Personal attention for a child in Manaus . . .

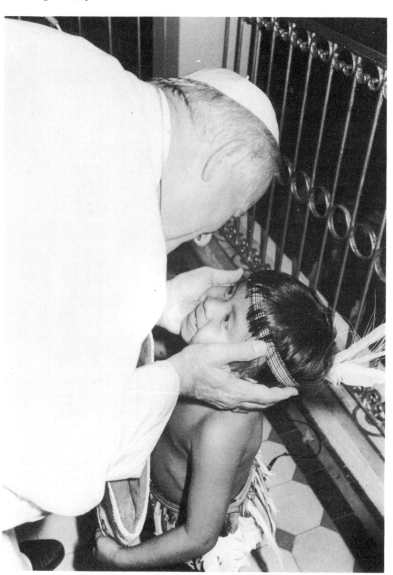

So the strategy of the visit to Brazil was in the end perfectly clear. The Brazilian bishops were confirmed in their social commitments, but John Paul provided a different rationale: he agreed with them and backed them up, but in the name of the social doctrine of the Church, not of liberation theology. At the same time they were warned that some of their methods are perilous if not deviant, and that closer collaboration with the Roman Curia is called for in the future. The message to the government, meanwhile, was that the social doctrine of the Church, applied systematically, is the only thing that can save it from a worse fate—and that time is running out fast.

. . . but the strain of continual demand for attention beginning to show.

Both sides were invited to share a vision. If the business of a prophet is not so much to predict the future as to interpret people to themselves, to remind them of convictions they had almost forgotten they possessed, then this royal progress had a prophetic aspect. It was certainly grandiose in conception and execution.

14   *The Family Synod*

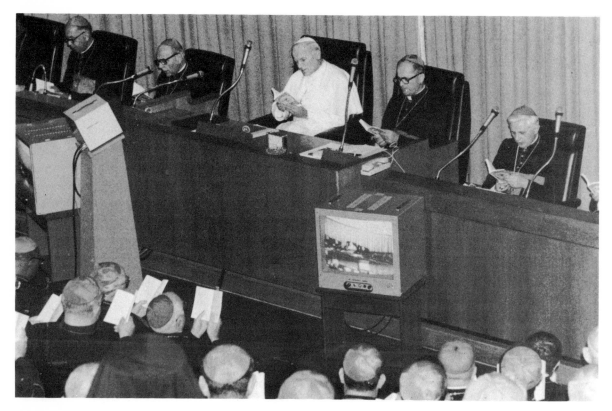

The opening of the Synod of Bishops on 29 September.

The Synod on 'The Role of the Christian Family in the Modern World' began with high hopes on 26 September and ended in confusion and a mood of frustration on 25 October. The move from optimism to pessimism may have been caused by exaggerated expectations on the part of the outsiders. The 216 Synod members, at any rate, emerged bravely smiling and said that the Synod had been a remarkably successful event. They had learned a great deal, especially in their discussion groups, and gained a keener sense of the universality of the Church. Observers wondered whether they were not simply whistling to keep their courage up.

The Synod fell into two distinct parts, one semi-public and encouraging, the other opaque and dismaying. It started so well. For the first two weeks its members reported on what was happening in their countries, made recommendations based on pastoral needs, and acknowledged the importance of listening to married couples on these matters. 'They must be listened to', said Cardinal Basil Hume of Westminster, 'first because they are the ministers of the sacrament, and second, because they alone have experienced the effects of the sacrament' (29 September).

Cardinal Basil Hume OSB,
Archbishop of Westminster.

The married, in short, are a 'theological source'. Most of the eleven language-based discussion groups reflected the same spirit of humble realism about human sexuality. This was the Synod's finest hour.

Five major themes emerged from these early discussions. The first was a plea for a 'positive approach' to sexuality and marriage. Bans and prohibitions did not help towards Christian living. The negative signposts needed to be replaced by positive ones. Cardinal Tomas O Fiaich, Primate of Ireland, made an interesting contribution on 30 September. He said:

Cardinal Tomas O Fiaich,
Archbishop of Armagh, Primate of
All Ireland.

*Some husbands find it difficult to express their love for their wives.
They are reticent about showing signs of affection. They think that to
show tenderness or emotion is soft or unmanly. They sometimes bring
the values that are admired in their place of work—strength, firmness,
competitiveness, decisiveness—into the home. They are not sensitive
enough to the differences in sexuality between male and female.*

This sounded a distinctly new note. It meant a recognition of the
equality of the unitive and procreative values of marriage. It was
a break with the bad tradition before Vatican II which made
having children the 'primary end' while 'the mutual comfort of
the spouses' (or 'remedy for concupiscence') was relegated to
the second place and seen as a concession to human weakness.
It also implied a different attitude to *Humanae Vitae*.

102

This was the second important theme of the Synod. Many fathers thought that the time had come for another look at the 1968 encyclical, not in order to subvert it, but to set it in a fresh context. For it was an undeniable fact that *Humanae Vitae* had not always been well understood or well received. Archbishop John R. Quinn of San Francisco, who spoke in the name of the US bishops, noted that this opposition was found 'even among those whose lives are otherwise outstanding in their Christian dedication, and among pastors whose learning, faith, discretion and dedication to the Church are beyond doubt' (29 September).

Cardinal Hume also spoke of those for whom 'natural methods of birth-control do not seem to be the only solution', and he added, 'It cannot just be said that these persons have failed to overcome their human frailty and weakness. Indeed, such persons are often good, conscientious and faithful sons and daughters of the Church. They just cannot accept that the use of artificial means of contraception in some circumstances is *intrinsice inhonestum*, as this latter has generally been understood' (29 September).

Doctrine and life, theology and pastoral practice, norms and values seem to have come adrift. What was to be done? Archbishop Quinn declared that 'the problem is not going to be solved merely by a reiteration of past formulations or by ignoring the fact of dissent'. It could only be tackled by starting a formal dialogue between the *magisterium* and Catholic theologians. This would involve first of all a listening phase which would include 'both those who support the Church's teaching and those who do not'. The proposed dialogue would be based on the principle of Pope Leo XIII: 'The Church has nothing to fear from the truth'. It was clear that the strategy of the US bishops was to look for solutions and further study *after* the Synod: such weighty and delicate matters could not be dealt with in a hectic four weeks and without the aid of theologians.

The third synodal theme was first touched upon by Archbishop Derek Worlock of Liverpool, also on 29 September. He dealt with marital breakdown. 'To these victims of misfortune,' he said, 'not necessarily of personal sin, or of sin that has not been forgiven, the Church must have a healing ministry of reconciliation'. His point was that people separate not because they are wicked but because they are desperate. Condemnations merely add to their distress. Some of them have already made second, stable marriages (even if only civilly) and have children. They seek admission to the sacraments, for their own sake and for the sake of the children. Archbishop Worlock put two questions to the Synod:

Archbishop Derek Worlock of Liverpool.

Is this spirit of repentance and desire for sacramental strength to be for ever frustrated? Can they be told only that they must reject their new responsibilities as a necessary condition for forgiveness and restorations to sacramental life?

That, he implied, would be a bleak and disappointing conclusion.

Finally, Archbishop Worlock answered the objection that to extend such a sacramental welcome to the divorced and remarried would be a cause of scandal to the faithful and a blow to the indissolubility of marriage. He based his answer on the experience of the National Pastoral Congress held in Liverpool

2–5 May. 'Those', he said, 'who vigorously uphold the Church's teaching on indissolubility, also ask for mercy and compassion for the repentant who have suffered irrevocable marital breakdown.' Many of the discussion groups echoed this plea and proposed a study of the practice of the Orthodox Churches in this matter.

The two remaining themes can be more briefly dealt with, though they were no less important. The first was the recognition that, as Bishop Robert Lebel of Valleyfield, Canada, put it, 'the feminist movement is a good thing and contains some Gospel values.' There was nothing particularly Christian about the traditional distinction of roles. Sharing domestic chores and child-care could bring the couple closer together. Archbishop Godefried Daneels said that the Church was in danger of losing women in the late twentieth century just as it had lost the working class in the nineteenth century. The discussion group presided over by Cardinal Hume said 'the Synod should encourage equality of rights for men and women in family life and, where sacred orders are not involved, in the organisation of the Church.' Despite the bracketing-out of ordination, this is a far-reaching principle.

Finally, African bishops, almost to a man, wanted greater freedom to take over into the liturgy some of their traditional marriage customs. 'Customary marriage', as it is called, takes place in stages, involves the two families and the whole community, and the idea that one can be married in a single moment of time when the vows are exchanged seems like a western (and colonialist) imposition. In India, where many marriages are mixed, the bishops wanted to be able to allow a double marriage ceremony.

But then came the disappointment. Everything that has so far been reported was made available through a reasonably efficient information service. On the first working day of the Synod, Bishop Agnellus Andrew, the Scottish Franciscan who is Vice-President of the Vatican Commission on the Media, had said that the information provided should reflect 'quickly, and in conformity with the truth, the course of the Synod's work'. He added that this was the will of the Synod and of the Holy Father.

In the end, all the decisions of the
Synod end up in the Pope's hands.

But half-way through the Synod this sensible principle was abandoned. The portcullis of silence dropped and the drawbridges were hauled up from the moment that the Synod began to discuss and vote upon the 'propositions' which embodied its 'advice' to the Pope. In the end there were 43 'propositions'. They were not officially published. No one could satisfactorily explain why. But the result was that the Synod members went home empty-handed and could only comment vaguely on an invisible, inaudible, inaccessible event.

Pope John Paul was present at the Synod as often as possible. He was seen to be taking notes and writing vigorously. In addition, he had lunch with groups of Synod members every day. At one of these lunches, on 20 October, Cardinal Emmett Carter, Archbishop of Toronto, assured the Pope that his continued presence had been a great help to all involved in the Synod. 'Why?' asked John Paul, surprised, 'I didn't say anything.' 'Precisely,' said Cardinal Carter, 'you didn't say anything. You could have intervened. You could have pulled a face or shown disapproval. But you did nothing of the kind. You left the Synod free.'

But if the Synod members claimed disingenuously that they did not know how the Pope was reacting during the Synod, his final address in the Sistine Chapel left them in no doubt about where he stood. All the optimistic 'openings' glimpsed by the Synod were systematically rejected. Where most observers saw the prospect of pastoral progress, John Paul saw only dangers. *Humanae Vitae* was reaffirmed in all its rigour. Theologians could help the *magisterium*, but not in the way suggested by Archbishop Quinn. Their task was to bring out 'the biblical foundation and so-called "personalistic" reasons for the doctrine'. Even the escape hatch of 'gradualness', which some had proposed, was carefully battened down. There can be no question of 'keeping the law merely as an ideal to be achieved in the future'.

The divorced and remarried were bluntly told that unless they repented and lived without scandal 'as brother and sister' they could not be admitted to the sacrament of reconciliation (penance) still less to the Eucharist. No mention was made of studying the practice of the Orthodox Churches (and it vanished from the propositions as well). Archbishop Worlock's two questions were answered with a resounding *niet*.

Nor did Bishop Lebel's optimistic remarks about the feminist movement find a sympathetic echo in John Paul's concluding address. To avoid distortion, the full text had better be given, in all the awkward stiffness of the official translation:

In words both opportune and persuasive the Synod has spoken of woman with reverence and a grateful spirit, especially of her dignity as a daughter of God, as a wife, and as a mother. It is commendably asked that women should not be forced to engage in external work, proper to a certain role, or, as they say, profession, but rather so that the family might be able to live rightly, that the mother might devote herself fully to the family.

Note that this was presented not as John Paul's own thoughts on the subject of women, but as the conclusion of the Synod.

No one should really have been surprised at this cold-shower ending to the Synod. For it was the peculiar misfortune of the 1980 Synod to be on a theme on which John Paul is an acknowledged expert and on which he has already pronounced many times. So the ordinary laws of collegiality could hardly apply, and the question inevitably arises: did John Paul really want or need 'advice and information' on this topic? (For that, according to its founder, Pope Paul VI, is the function of a Synod.) If the answer is 'no', the whole purpose of the Synod is transformed.

It is no longer a matter of pastors from all over the world sharing with the Pope the benefit of their own experience and helping him to decide what to do for the good of the whole Church: it becomes a pre-programmed celebration of the unity of the world's bishops gathered round the Pope. All the synodal side-shows—the carefully selected lay 'auditors' with their enthusiastic endorsement of natural family planning, the lectures by doctors one-sidedly committed to such methods, the family demonstration in St Peter's Square in the rain on 12 October—confirmed that the Synod simply had to give the right answers. The appearance of a genuine quest in the first two weeks proved to be an illusion.

All of which poses problems for honest bishops. They do not wish to be disloyal to the Pope; but they also believe that they have a duty of loyalty to their people. The secrecy which descended upon the Synod allowed assertions of unanimity to be made, which had not been verified in the more open discussions of the first two weeks. Cardinal Hume's dream was realised, if not in the way he had intended:

And I saw in my dream a vision. It was a vision of the Church. I saw a fortress, strong and upstanding. Every stranger approaching seemed to those who defended it to be an enemy to be repelled; from that fortress the voices of those outside could not be heard.

(14 October)

The Synod on the family had been turned into the fortress Synod.

15 *To the Land of Luther*

Arriving at Cologne in November –
the crowd included some
compatriots.

At Butzweiler Hof near Cologne is a deserted airfield, formerly
manned by the Belgian air force. There John Paul II said his first
Mass on German soil. But before he arrived the airfield was
carefully searched for unexploded bombs and mines left over
from the war. That seemed an apt symbol for John Paul's
journey to Germany: his path was littered with potentially
explosive material, and the story of the visit is an account of how
he defused and dismantled it. But that was far from evident in
advance. There were moments when it was touch and go.

The date of the visit was determined by the 700th anniversary of
the death of St Albert the Great, Dominican, scholar, bishop,
master of St Thomas Aquinas in Paris. His body lies in the
Dominican church of St Andrew, just three minutes away from
the cathedral in Cologne. John Paul has a Polish passion for
anniversaries. Without such a pretext, it would have made no
sense to go to Germany in November, when rain and bitter
winds could be confidently expected. They duly happened. But
Albert raised other and more serious problems. A lady
theologian showed, texts in hand, that Albert the Great held a
number of curious ideas. He believed, for example, that a
girl-child was the result of an unsuccessful attempt to produce a
boy. In addition to being anti-feminist, he was also said to be
anti-semitic. How would John Paul box his way out of that
corner?

Of much greater importance was the fact that the ecumenical
atmosphere in Germany had been soured just before John Paul
was due to come. The German bishops were largely to blame.
They had rapidly commissioned a series of three booklets to

prepare the visit. One of them was a brief history of the Church in Germany. It contained 24 pages unwisely entrusted to Professor Remigius Bäumer who dealt with the Reformation. He presented Martin Luther as a man 'whose uncontrollable anger and polemical spirit blinded him to Catholic truth'. His marriage to an ex-nun was described as 'sacrilegious and stained by fornication'. The condemnation of Luther was 'inevitable'—a point that is disputed by many scholars. Uproar ensued. Indignant letters were written to the press. The German Bishops hastily backtracked and claimed that they had not had time to read the offending chapter. It seemed a lame excuse.

At the open-air Mass at Butzweiler Hof.

Meeting scientists and students in Cologne cathedral.

While the bishops were reeling under this blow, some 130 theologians, including Hans Küng and Johannes Baptist Metz, delivered a letter to the Papal Nuncio in Bonn on the Sunday before John Paul arrived. They put six provocative questions to the Pope concerning the Church's commitment to the poor of the third world, the scandal of the arms race, ecumenism, the admission to the sacraments of the divorced and remarried, the ordination of women and married men, and freedom for theological research. Since John Paul's views on the last three topics were not exactly a mystery, here was another noisily ticking time-bomb.

Finally, and most pervasively, there was genuine anxiety about the first encounter between the Germans and a Polish Pope. Even if the horrors of the Nazi occupation in Poland had been officially forgiven, they could not be entirely forgotten and they had affected Karol Wojtyla in his most formative years. He was twenty-four when Cracow was 'liberated' in January 1945. Conversely, many Germans had settled in the West after being driven from their homes in Silesia. Almost one-third of contemporary Poland consists of land filched from Germany and handed over to the Poles as 'the recovered territories'. Some German *revanchistes* have never accepted this post-war humiliation. One false step here, and the whole visit could have been wrecked.

But all the gloomy prognostications were routed. John Paul rose to the challenge—and enjoyed it.

On Saturday 15 November the cathedral in Cologne was filled with four thousand scientists and academics (filled out by students and high school pupils) who listened to a lecture on St Albert the Great. 'The content of Albert's work', John Paul roundly declared, 'was often time-bound, but his method of uniting faith and reason is still exemplary for us today.' This neat move enabled him to ignore all the difficulties raised by Albert's writings, from which he gave not a single quotation, and to treat him as a symbolic figure. Albert the Great points the way to a positive partnership between science and faith. This is one of the favourite themes of John Paul, and in his mind Germany was the right place to develop it. Nowhere else had he addressed 'scientists' (*Wissenschaftler*). In his mental map of the world, Germany is the home of *Geist,* of science and philosophy. His second thesis had been on Max Scheler, who had been professor in Cologne in the 1920s. Germany is the country which he finds intellectually most congenial, and where his philosophical style is most appreciated.

John Paul said that 'there can be no conflict between science and faith provided science remains faithful to its methods.' Moreover, recent developments have made a re-thinking of the relationship urgent. The whole ecological movement, for example, puts a question-mark against the idea of 'progress': is any price worth paying for it? Again, the human sciences of psychology and sociology have sometimes abandoned any concern for 'meaning' and 'truth', so that the very notion of 'reason' is put in jeopardy. Meanwhile, the various ideologies which claimed to satisfy the hunger for 'meaning' have been discredited.

Then John Paul moved over to the attack. The 'crisis of ideologies' gives the Church its chance. Its enemies used to hurl at it the slogans of Reason, Freedom and Progress. But today it is the Church which defends Reason (against various irrationalisms), Freedom (against tyrannies) and Progress (against pessimism). 'A new alliance is needed between faith and science', cried John Paul, 'and a new humanism for the third millennium.' Faced with this vision of the Church as the champion of science and of Christianity as a renewed cultural force, the critics of John Paul seemed to be pettifogging and mean-minded. In the glittering Herkules-Saal of the Residenz in Munich the following Wednesday, he made a similar plea for a new alliance between the Church and artists, faith and culture. His project is nothing less than a one-man cultural revolution. These questions seemed to interest him more than inner-Church affairs.

But of course he found time for ecumenism. On the morning of Sunday 16 November John Paul was in Osnabrück, the most northerly point of his German visit. Before the war only five per cent of the population in this region was Catholic. Refugees and immigrant workers have pushed this figure up to fifteen per cent. But it remains a minority Church. The Catholics of North Germany have special reason to be grateful to the Evangelicals, who lent them their churches until they could build their own. 'In the last decades', John Paul said, 'the ecumenical movement has shown how close you are to your Evangelical brothers and how much you have in common with them when both you and they live honourably and coherently according to faith in Our Lord Jesus Christ.' Did that suggest that there were dishonourable and incoherent versions of the faith on offer? John Paul did not say: but he had planted a niggling doubt. But on the whole he was encouraging. He sees ecumenism first and foremost as a spiritual attitude. He looks at the distant scene, not the next step. 'Eventually', he said, 'the Spirit will show us the way to spiritual and visible unity.' In a splendid phrase he remarked that 'all ecumenical conversation, all joint prayer and action, are already enfolded in the prayer of Christ "that all may be one".'

These heartening signals meant that the meeting with the nine leaders of the German Evangelical Church (EED) gained in importance. It took place the following day in the chapter-house of the diocesan museum in Mainz at eight o'clock in the morning. Everyone waited for the outcome of this historic meeting with baited breath. Would John Paul come off the ecumenical fence? Would he say something sympathetic about Luther to offset the gaffe made by the German bishops?

Yet again, John Paul revealed his talent for the unexpected. He shifted the ground of the question. He began with a reference to Luther that reflected neither praise nor blame, and could conceivably have been no more than a literary conceit. Luther, he noted, had been in Rome as a pilgrim in 1510–1511; and now in 1980, he, the Pope, had come to Germany as a pilgrim. Most of his speech was devoted to a commentary on the Epistle to the Romans, which Luther had described as 'the heart of the New Testament'. John Paul rehearsed and made his own most of the favourite Lutheran themes: 'We have all sinned. We cannot therefore judge each other. Jesus Christ is the salvation of us all: he is the One Mediator. Through him the Father grants us pardon, justification, grace and eternal life. We must all confess these truths.'

For a wild moment one wondered whether John Paul was on the verge of announcing that he had become a Lutheran. But this prospect was quickly dispelled when he produced a quotation from Luther's 1516–1517 lectures on Romans. Luther had said that 'justifying faith involves faith not only in the person of Christ but faith in "what Christ is".' John Paul spelled out this mysterious phrase and said that Luther included in faith in 'what Christ is' an acceptance of 'the Church and its authentic preaching of the Gospel'. Perhaps it was unfair of him to set the early, still Catholic Luther against the late, post-break Luther. But undoubtedly he had touched on the most crucial issue in Catholic-Evangelical relations. Is faith in the Church to be regarded as the necessary extension of faith in Christ? Or can

Mass at Fulda: recalling St Boniface.

faith in Christ be maintained while holding that the Church is a human institution in constant need of reform? Having hinted at this central question, John Paul observed that dialogue must proceed on these matters, and that yet another joint commission would be set up. But there could be no immediate concessions on inter-communion because 'only full unity allows us to gather round the table of the Lord with one heart and one faith.'

The Evangelicals were somewhat non-plussed by this wholly unexpected approach. Half their Lutheran clothes had been stealthily removed while they were not looking. Their prepared

115

shopping-list, with its sensible proposals on mixed marriages, intercommunion and common ecumenical services on Sundays, now seemed very ordinary indeed. Those concerned with the 'next step' in ecumenical relations had been up-staged. It seemed merely petty to raise such troublesome points on a cold November morning when so lofty and spiritual a vision of unity had been dangled before their eyes. Bishop Eduard Lohse, President of the EKD Council, remarked afterwards that 'the way the Pope spoke to each one of us personally created a good climate—a climate of mutual listening.' But he was evidently a little bewildered and could point to no practical step forwards. It seemed rather pathetic to be reduced to saying that the meeting was a great success because it had run on for ten minutes over the agreed hour. But the decisive point for the future was that John Paul had spoken dispassionately of Luther as a witness to Christian living.

A similar charity, however, was not extended to dissident Catholic theologians. There was a meeting with carefully screened theologians in Fulda during which John Paul declared that 'the liberty of scientific theology is qualified by its bond with the Church, recognised by the Concordat, which remains a model for today, despite certain conflicts.' The Concordat was signed with Hitler in 1933, and it permitted the deposition of Hans Küng, who was the invisible interlocutor throughout the visit. (Küng was in the United States, fulfilling previous engagements.) But apart from this address, there were many other glancing references to recent theological controversies. Talking to the scientists in Cologne Cathedral, John Paul spoke of the need for science to be 'free for the truth'. This was an anti-Marxist point, directed against the Communist manipulation of science. But obviously it raised questions nearer home. John Paul anticipated this thrust. 'The Church', he said, 'wants independent theological research.' Scattered applause greeted this apparent concession to Küng. But the sentence had not yet been completed. John Paul went on to add that this 'independent theological research' was also bound to respect 'the truths of faith and the needs of the People of God.' The applause was even more enthusiastic.

In Fulda on Monday evening the sermon was devoted to the theme of clerical celibacy, not surprisingly, since he had before him a cathedral full of bishops, priests and seminarians. The tomb of St Boniface, the ninth century Devonian Benedictine who evangelised Germany and is its official patron, was conveniently to hand to add the dimension of history. Taking as his text the phrase of John's Gospel, 'not servants but friends', John Paul told his clerical congregation: 'Christ asks a lot of you, but he asks it as a friend. His desire is that in the spirit of the evangelical counsels you should have hands and hearts free for friendship with Jesus Christ.' The fruit of this celibate friendship with Christ, he went on, would be friendship with each other, through friendship with their bishops: immense applause greeted this hopeful statement. It was another instance of drawing disciplinary conclusions from a spiritual principle, for, as he added, 'unity with the bishops and with the successor of St Peter is the condition without which friendship with Jesus Christ cannot be realised.'

Thus the way was prepared for a direct and would-be devastating attack on Küng's view that the denial of the right of priests to marry is a denial of human rights within the Church. 'Christ teaches us', said John Paul, 'that man has a right to his greatness, a right to that which transcends him, for in that way his true value is shown and the path of grace is opened up. Our strength is not our own but is the gift of the Spirit. Follow your vocation, definitively and for ever, and grace will be granted to you.' Does this mean that there are no human rights left in the Church? It does not, but John Paul defined them carefully: 'Human persons and the Church itself have the right to know that this inherited certainty [about priestly celibacy] will not in any way be weakened, and young men have the right not to have obstacles put in their path in this matter.' Rapturous applause from the assembled seminarians. John Paul had won another round.

The political risk inherent in being a Polish Pope in Germany was warded off with surprising ease. On Sunday evening, 16 November, which is peak viewing time also in East Germany, where 70 per cent of the population can receive West German TV, he said Mass at the USAF air base at Finthen-bei-Mainz. There was a 'never again war' passage which gained special poignancy considering who was speaking and where: 'The frightful destruction of the last war, the indescribable sufferings of so many, the sheer contempt for man—that must never again be repeated in this generation, never again, either in this continent or elsewhere.' Enthusiastic applause. The applause was even more enthusiastic when John Paul referred to the current meeting in Madrid which was supposed to be monitoring the implementation of the Final Act of the Helsinki Conference on Security and Co-operation. It had strongly asserted human rights, including religious freedom. John Paul said, his voice rising to a crescendo, that he hoped that 'the effective application of these principles about the rights of man and nations, no matter how small, will banish every form of imperialism, aggression, colonialism and exploitation.' In case there should be any doubt about what kind of imperialism and which country he had in mind, he immediately added: 'I say this as the son of a nation that has suffered greatly for hundreds of years and so has been obliged to defend the rights of man.' Vast and prolonged applause, to which some residual guilt-feelings may have contributed.

The sermon ended with a prayer for 'those brothers in the faith whose rights are infringed, for those who are oppressed, for those who are not allowed religious liberty'. The prayer was made even more specific: 'We also pray for your fellow-countrymen who remain heroically faithful. May we all remain faithful. May God give us the grace of strength, especially in the hour of trial.' Was this a denial of the existence and legitimacy of the German Democratic Republic? It could be read that way. What else did the reference to 'fellow-countrymen' mean? On the night, these remarks were applauded to the darkened skies. Though their long-term effect can only be 'destabilising', they flattered German national sentiment and meant that from then on the Polish Pope was assured of popular approval.

It remained only to go to Bavaria, a traditionally Catholic *Land*, where sentimentality always threatens. There John Paul visited the Marian shrine of Altötting, near the Czech border, talked with 'artists and media people' in the Residenz, and finally with old people in the cathedral in Munich with its double onion towers. The last meeting showed him at his best. His address was a prose poem which compared old age with the season of autumn. He could have been thinking of himself, now sixty.

Preaching at Cologne: recalling St Albert the Great.

The senses are less acute, and the body no longer obeys the mind so readily. New information is less easily assimilated, and the memory begins to play tricks. The world of economics and politics becomes baffling and strange, and even the Church is no longer what it used to be. Death itself takes on the form of a consolation and a longed-for release from imprisonment. For this world, concluded John Paul, is not our true and definitive home. It was deeply felt, beautifully expressed, profoundly Slav in its melancholy, and entirely appropriate.

Freezing conditions at the Theresienwiese, but huge crowds still came to an open-air Mass.

But there had been another event on Wednesday 19 November, final day of the visit to Germany, that was unplanned and utterly astonishing. The Mass in the Theresienwiese, a vast park in the heart of Munich where the October beer-festival is held, was dedicated to the theme of 'youth'. The weather had improved a little. Patches of blue-sky could be seen, but the temperature was sub-zero. 600,000 frozen Bavarians of all ages heard John Paul exhort young men to consider a vocation to the priesthood. They should refuse the temptation of drugs, alcohol, sensual pleasure, sects and utopian political ideologies. They should reject the notion of 'provisional' commitments. Women were barely mentioned, except as possible recruits for religious orders.

120

After the Mass a young woman, Barbara Engl, President of the Munich Association of Catholic Youth, stepped forward to deliver her address of welcome. She had thrown away her officially approved text and said frankly that, having listened to the sermon, she still had difficulties with the Church in West Germany. 'Young people', she said, 'have the feeling that the Church is more interested in perpetuating divisions with other Christians rather than stressing what brings us together. They find that their concern for friendship, sexuality and partnership receives only negative answers.'

John Paul seems to be dogged by women. In Washington it was Sr Theresa Kane who told him what he did not want to know. In Cologne, a banner exhorted him to 'go and see Aunt Emma, who has words to say to you in the kitchen.' And now it was Frau Engl who would not shut up: 'Many young people cannot understand why the Church should insist so strongly on celibacy for its priests, when there is such a manifest lack of priests, especially young chaplains for universities and high schools. Nor can they understand why a greater sharing of women in the Church should be ruled out.' John Paul listened with head in hands. He was tired and not gruntled. If he had a reply in mind, it did not come, for he was immediately hustled away by an embarrassed Cardinal Jozef Ratzinger, Archbishop of Munich. The Pope was behind schedule, as usual.

So in the end John Paul was not the only one in Germany who could take people by surprise. The previous day, in Fulda, he had denounced those who spoke of Germany as a 'post-Christian society'. From the tomb of St Boniface, bishop and martyr, where German Christianity really began, he announced that 'a new era is dawning in Christian history, thanks to your witness.' So the purpose of his visit to Germany was, as he saw it, to roll back the tide of secularisation and modernity. But Barbara Engl's brief remarks put a question-mark against this grandiose project: had John Paul invented a Germany of the historical imagination and failed to speak to the country as it really was, or will be?

16 *Any Other Business*

Archbishop Lefebvre, the
75-year-old leader of the
traditionalist dissidents . . .

A year—even a papal year—is an arbitrary segment of time. Much was accomplished in 1980 and for John Paul the pace was dizzy-making. He even managed to slip in another encyclical, *Dives in misericordia*, dated the first Sunday in Advent. But many problems remain unsolved. Some of them will be briefly reported on here.

The dissident traditionalist, Archbishop Marcel Lefebvre, persisted in provocative gestures. On Easter Monday he celebrated Mass in a disused church near the Venice railway station and denounced, yet again, the unholy alliance of Church

. . . at the 'illicit' ordination of priests at Ecône on 29 June.

and revolution. His supporters continued their occupation of the church of St Nicolas du Chardonnet in Paris. On 29 June there were more priestly ordinations at the Lefebvre seminary at Ecône in Switzerland. Like his earlier ordinations they were, in the language of canon law, 'valid but illicit'. So before there can be a formal reconciliation, Lefebvre will have to give an undertaking to desist from such actions and declare that he now accepts the Second Vatican Council as part of the authentic teaching of the Church. That would not be easy for him. It would involve eating a lot of previous words. But there was distinct evidence that Lefebvre, who was 75 on 5 November, was waiting for a sign from Pope John Paul. On 2 November he said that there was 'a new and more favourable atmosphere in the Vatican'. No sign came, however, and the Vatican press office issued its ritual denial.

Others who were waiting for a sign included the 4,000 or so priests whose requests for laicisation had been blocked from the start of the pontificate. The Pope was said to be reviewing the cases personally. New norms were promised. But from June onwards a steady trickle of laicisations began, according to the old rules: however, this was a false dawn, merely a way of dealing with the backlog of cases. The new policy was eventually enshrined in a letter from Cardinal Franjo Seper, prefect of the Congregation for the Doctrine of the Faith, which accompanied the formal statement of the new norms. Both documents were dated 14 October, but have still not been 'officially' published.

That their intention is to make laicisation more difficult and more rare is not in doubt, but canon lawyers wondered how they would actually be applied. It will be difficult for most priests to provide 'solid and substantial proofs' that they were 'not free' at the time of ordination, and the likelihood is that seminary rectors and spiritual directors, who alone could give such evidence, will be dead or of failing memory by the time they need to be consulted. Nor was it easy to interpret the clause about 'those who have abandoned the priesthood a long time ago and seek to put right a situation from which they cannot free themselves'. How long is a long time? How inextricable does the situation—which presumably means civil marriage and children—have to be?

Theologians were more struck by the parallel that Seper's letter makes between marriage and ordination. Marriage vows and priestly vows are placed on the same level. But as one French theologian remarked: 'it is no doubt true that marriage is the sacrament of love, but you cannot say that ordination is the sacrament of celibacy.' A priest is ordained to the ministry and for the community. Celibacy may be a condition required by the Latin Church, but it cannot be made an essential condition of the priesthood itself, for that would rule out married oriental priests and the ex-Episcopalians, whose 'reconciliation' was surprisingly announced in California in August.

The Society of Jesus has also been the object of John Paul's attentions. In September 1979 he said that he had received disquieting reports about the activities of some of the world's 27,000 Jesuits. They were departing from their tradition of absolute loyalty to the *magisterium* and falling into secularisation and slackness. Paul VI had issued similar broadsides. The difference was that now words tended to be followed by deeds. Fr Pedro Arrupe, General of the Jesuits, wrote a stiff letter to his men to say that 'warnings from three successive popes' (John Paul I had also prepared a document just before his death) 'could not be ignored', and that there would have to be an immediate and tangible response. That was on 17 October 1979, feast of the North American Martyrs. Individual Jesuits began to feel the heat. Fr William Callahan in Washington was ordered to give up his advocacy of the ordination of women and then shunted round from diocese to diocese in search of a well-disposed bishop. In May Fr Robert Drinan was told by Arrupe, acting on papal orders, not to stand for re-election to the American Congress. It was little consolation that John Paul was at the same time honouring Jesuits by making them, against all precedent, archbishops of important sees (Milan and Strasbourg), for they were thus in a sense 'removed' from their order. 'The Pope', said a Gregorian Professor, 'is kissing us to death.'

Fr Pedro Arrupe SJ: the General ordered to stay at his post.

There was no causal link between these events and Arrupe's attempt to resign. News of this came out only in August, but he had been sounding opinion from early spring. If Arrupe were to resign, he would have to call a General Congregation to elect his successor. But a General Congregation cannot be improvised: a whole orderly sequence of meetings and elections has to take place on the local level first. Arrupe was poised to set the complicated process in motion when he had a ten-minute meeting with John Paul who told him not to summon a General Congregation because 'it would not be opportune at this time for the good of the Society or the good of the Church'. Arrupe accepted this decision 'in a filial spirit'. For the time being he cannot resign.

It is easier to state the facts than to interpret them. John Paul could have meant to show his confidence in Arrupe's leadership in order to dispel the gossip which suggested the contrary. Or

The Pope from Poland.

he may be happier with the General he knows rather than with some hazardous newcomer. Or—the most likely hypothesis—he may not want another General Congregation because it would inevitably mean much unfettered discussion, some of it in public, on the present state of the Church; and it is not beyond the bounds of possibility that the Jesuits would offer an account of the crisis which differs from that of the Pope. In this way a General Congregation of the Jesuits would be a threat and perhaps an embarrassment.

Finally, one must note the most important, yet most elusive, way in which John Paul 'changed the world' in 1980. Throughout the summer and autumn events in Poland, with the wave of strikes, the recognition of the unofficial union, Solidarity, and the replacement of Mr Edward Gierek by Mr Stanislaw Kania as the first secretary of the Polish Communist Party, John Paul remained diplomatically silent. He confined himself to asking for prayers for Poland. But he was following the situation with intense interest, and could be regarded as 'Poland's absent leader'. Unless there had been a Polish pope, and unless he had been to Poland in June 1979, the Polish events would not have happened in quite the same way. His election and his visit gave a boost to the morale of the country and acted as an informal plebiscite on the question, who really rules Poland? This was the basis on which the union between workers and intellectuals could go forward. They were determined this time to avoid the usual Polish practice of making an heroic gesture that changed nothing. John Paul's discreet role was recognized in that Mr Lech Walesa, leader of Solidarity, expressed a desire to go to Rome 'to thank the Pope'. It is also noteworthy that Cardinal Stefan Wyszynski, the 79-year-old primate of Poland, arrived at the Vatican on 24 October and stayed for two weeks for 'consultations' about which nothing was ever released. Throughout this time there were threats of further strikes and hints of Russian intervention. The Polish story, like everything else in this book, is incomplete.

There will be another *Papal Year*.